# On the Uses of Anaphoric Forms in Chinese Discourses

# 汉语篇章回指研究

CUI Yuzhen

崔玉珍　著

DOCTOR OF PHILOSOPHY
CITY UNIVERSITY OF HONG KONG
APRIL 2011

南开大学出版社
天　津

图书在版编目(CIP)数据

汉语篇章回指研究 ：英文 / 崔玉珍著. —天津：南开大学出版社，2014.8
ISBN 978-7-310-04684-3

Ⅰ. ①汉… Ⅱ. ①崔… Ⅲ. ①汉语—语法—研究—英语 Ⅳ. ①H146

中国版本图书馆 CIP 数据核字(2014)第 232147 号



南开大学出版社出版发行
出版人:孙克强
地址:天津市南开区卫津路 94 号 邮政编码:300071
营销部电话:(022)23508339 23500755
营销部传真:(022)23508542 邮购部电话:(022)23502200
*
天津泰宇印务有限公司印刷
全国各地新华书店经销
*
2014 年 8 月第 1 版 2014 年 8 月第 1 次印刷
230×170 毫米 16 开本 12 印张 200 千字
定价:26.00 元

如遇图书印装质量问题，请与本社营销部联系调换，电话:(022)23507125

# TABLE OF CONTENTS

# Chapter 1 Introduction

## 1.1 Understanding Chinese Anaphoric Forms

This thesis is to deal chiefly with the uses of different Chinese anaphoric forms. Anaphora has been a hot topic in linguistics, especially in Chinese linguistics, for it involves a complex set of linguistic issues such as discourse coherence, discourse interpretations, natural language processing, and so on.

The most intriguing issue in anaphora is how to explain distinctive behaviors of different anaphoric forms. As is known, there are many kinds of anaphoric forms in Chinese, including full NPs, zero pronouns, overt pronouns, and so on. Exactly how different anaphoric forms are deployed in discourse attracts the attention of many researchers from different theoretical persuasions.

Generally speaking, in connected discourse, a discourse entity can be referred back to by another entity with the same or a different referring expression in subsequent text. Such a phenomenon is termed **anaphora. In anaphora**, the entity being referred back to by another entity is termed **antecedent** and the other entity referring back to the preceding entity is termed **anaphor**. We can say that there is an anaphoric link between the antecedent and the anaphor. Since anaphor can vary in form as referring expressions, the term **anaphoric form** is used to refer to the varying referring expressions. Let me illustrate this with the following example.

(1.1) a. Tangmingde$_i$ jinghuang de wang wai pao,

b. Ø$_i$ zhuang dao yi ge dahan$_j$ de shen shang,

c. ta$_i$ kan qing le na ren$_j$ de mei yan,

d. Ø$_i$ ren chu na ren$_j$ shi shui.（Chen (1991): 182）[①]

"Tangmingde was running out scarily, and collided into one big fellow. He saw the man's eyes, and recognizes who that man is."

In the above example, where there are four clauses (a-c), the entity *Tangmingde* is referred back to a number of times by different entities in the subsequent text: a zero pronoun Ø in (1.1b), a third-person pronoun *ta* in (1.1c), and a zero pronoun Ø again in (1.1d), which is indexed by the subscript letter "I". Thus we can say that the entity *Tangmingde* and the other entities referring back to it constitute an anaphoric chain: *Tangmingde* - Ø - *ta* - Ø, with *Tangmingde* being the antecedent of the zero pronoun in (1.1b), the zero pronoun in (1.1b) being the antecedent of the third-person pronoun ta in (1.1c), and *ta* in (1.1c) the antecedent of the zero pronoun in (1.1d).

There is another anaphoric chain the example (1.1) which is indexed by the subscript letter j: it is between the entity *yi ge dahan* (one big fellow) in (1.1b), *na ren* (that man) in (1.1c), and *na ren* (that man) in (1.1d).

As shown in example (1.1), there can be many different anaphoric forms. The referent *Tangmingde* is mentioned throughout (1.1a-d) but is encoded by different anaphoric forms: a zero pronoun Ø in (1.1b), the third-person pronoun *ta* in (1.1c), and another zero pronoun Ø again in (1.1d). Another referent *yi ge dahan* (one big fellow) is encoded by the same anaphoric form in (1.1c & d): a descriptive NP *na ren* (that man). Given the varied forms available in languages such as Mandarin Chinese, two questions naturally rise: in what kind of contexts should a particular kind of anaphoric form be used? What is the difference between different anaphoric forms?

There are a variety of approaches with different proposals being made to account for the use of different anaphoric forms. Accessibility Theory (AT),

① This thesis will use Ø to stand for zero anaphor in Chinese, and use the subscript letter to signal the anaphoric relation between an antecedent and an anaphor.

Centering Theory (CT), and Discourse Representative Theory (DRT) are the representative approaches in the previous research, which all seem to try to interpret anaphoric forms from a universal perspective and have inspired research on interpreting anaphoric forms in Chinese discourses.

Briefly speaking, Accessibility Theory chiefly proposes that different anaphoric forms are linguistic markers for different degrees of accessibility of antecedents (Cf. Keenan & Comrie (1977), Givón (1983), Ariel (1990, 1994, 2008), Gundel et al. (1993), etc.). Centering Theory argues that the focus of attention (the $C_b$ in CT) of an utterance is most possibly realized as the pronominal form (Cf. Grosz, Joshi, and Weinstein (1983, 1986, 1995), Walker (1998), Poesio et al. (2000), etc.). And Discourse Representative Theory attempts to suggest different accessibility conditions for different anaphoric forms to access the antecedents (Cf. Kamp (1981), Kamp & Reyle (1993), Asher (1993), etc.).

Although those three kinds of theories on anaphor interpretations seem to take very different approaches, they actually share some common features. They all contend, for example, that the anaphoric link between the antecedent and the anaphor is an accessible process and that the antecedent in a successful anaphoric link is accessible for the anaphor. The main difference among the three theories is that DRT appears to pay more attention to what entities are accessible for an anaphor, while AT and CT are concerned with how accessible an entity it is for an anaphor.

Admittedly, AT, CT, and DRT all are influential theories and have proposed many brilliant ideas for the interpretations on different anaphoric forms. But they are not free of problems. DRT cannot differentiate different uses of anaphoric forms with the accessibility conditions. AT cannot rightly determine the degree of accessibility of the antecedent and give an explicit correlation between the accessibility of the antecedent and the anaphoric forms. CT only shows its interests on the potential of the $C_b$ of an utterance being the pronominal expression and leaves out other uses of anaphoric forms.

Below is an illustration with the example (1.1).

As discussed earlier, there are two anaphoric chains in (1.1) shown below.

(1.2) *Tangmingde* in (1.1a) - Ø in (1.1b) – *ta* in (1.1c) – Ø in (1.1d)

Anaphoric Link: 

(1.3) *yi ge dahan* in (1.1b) – *na ren* in (1.1c) - *na ren* in (1.1d)

Anaphoric Link: 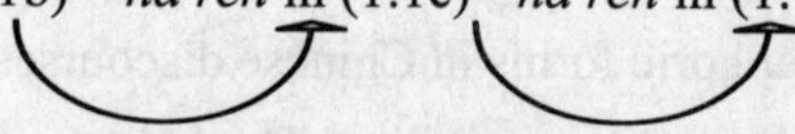

Let us firstly have a close look at the interpretations of AT on example (1.1). According to the proposal of AT, the degree of accessibility of *Tangmingde* in (1.1a) should be the same as that of *ta* in (1.1c) but different from that of Ø in (1.1b) due to the different behaviors of anaphoric forms: *Tangmingde* in (1.1a) and *ta* in (1.1c) both are referred back by the zero pronoun, while Ø in (1.1b) is referred back by the overt pronoun *ta*. But on the other hand, the degrees of accessibility of *Tangmingde* in (1.1a), Ø in (1.1b), and *ta* in (1.1c) should be the same, in that they all have the same behaviors in terms of the distance, the competition, the saliency, and the unity which are four factors to determinc the accessibility of the antecedent in AT. Hence there is a paradox in the interpretations of AT on the anaphoric forms of example (1.1), and the use of different, rather than identical, Chinese anaphoric forms in (1.2) cannot be rightly explained by AT.

Centering Theory is chiefly concerned with the center of utterance $C_b$ and its realized expressions. According to the proposals of CT, all entities in (1.2) are the $C_b$ of the utterance in which they occur respectively, and they can consequently be realized as a pronominal expression. But there are two kinds of pronominal expressions in (1.2), namely the zero pronoun and the overt pronoun *ta*, CT cannot explain the use of different Chinese anaphoric forms with pronominal expressions. On the other hand, there are anaphoric forms, such as the descriptive NP *na ren* in (1.3), which don't serve as the Cb. CT offers no explanation on their uses.

As far as Discourse Representation Theory is concerned, all entities in the anaphoric chain (1.2) or (1.3) are regarded as the discourse referents which occur in the same discourse representation structure. Hence all antecedents in (1.2) or in (1.3) are accessible for their anaphors based on the proposals of DRT. But DRT cannot tell why the anaphoric forms differ in different contexts.

Thus, even with all thee major theories of anaphora, distinctive behaviors of different Chinese anaphoric forms have not been thoroughly interpreted so far, though the existing research has posed a number of proposals to account for that. Thus, this thesis will set out to analyze the mechanisms of Chinese anaphora and attempts to interpret and explain the workings of all major types of anaphoric forms in Chinese discourses.

## 1.2 Taxonomy of Anaphora

Even though there has been a lot of research on anaphora, the definition of anaphora varies for different researchers. There are mainly three different kinds of views on anaphora in the literature.

1) The antecedent and the anaphor of an anaphora are NPs and co-referential (Cf. G. Hirst (1981), Chen (1987), Florian Jaeger (1999), Huang (2000), Shen (2000), etc.).

2) The antecedent and the anaphor of an anaphora are NPs but not necessarily co-referential. (Cf. Evans (1977, 1980, 1982), Quine (1960), Parsons (1978), Cooper (1979), Engdah (1986), Kadmon (1987, 1990), Lappin (1989), Heim (1990), Neale (1990), van der Does (1993), Lappin and Francez (1994), Chierchia (1995), etc.)

3) The antecedent and the anaphor of an anaphora can be NPs or other expressions such as Verb Phrase, Adjective Phrase, and so on (Cf. Kamp & Reyle (1993), Asher (1993), Peterson (1997), Smith (2003), etc.).

This thesis will focus on Chinese anaphora whose antecedent and anaphor are both NPs, which is actually the second kind of view we just discussed on anaphora. Such kind of Chinese anaphora will be called **Chinese NP anaphora** hereafter. ①

① In some previous research, the term **NP anaphora** is used to refer to an anaphora whose anaphor is a noun phrase (see Chen 1987, Liao 1992, J. Xu 2002, etc.) This thesis re-defines the concept **NP anaphora** as the anaphora whose antecedent and anaphor are both noun phrases. The anaphora whose anaphor is a noun phrase will be called **noun phrase anaphora in order** to differentiate these two.

There are many different kinds of anaphoric forms in Chinese NP anaphora, because scholars have tried to classify them and often with different categories or schemes.

Liao (1986), Chen (1987), Huang (1994), J. Xu (2002), Hu (2007) all classify Chinese anaphoric forms into three kinds: zero anaphor, pronoun anaphors, and noun anaphors. Zero anaphor refers to an empty pronoun. A pronoun anaphor refers to the anaphor which is an overt pronoun that usually refers to the third-person and is realized as a pronoun *ta*. And a noun anaphor refers to the anaphor which is a noun phrase.

In the field of general anaphoric studies, Ariel (1990) provides a detailed classification which distinguishes sixteen kinds of anaphors in English: Extremely High Accessibility Markers, Cliticized pronoun, Unstressed pronoun, Stressed pronoun, Stressed pronoun + gesture, Proximal demonstrative (+ NP), Distal demonstrative (+ NP), Proximal demonstrative + modifier, Distal demonstrative + modifier, First name, Last name, Short definite description, Long definite description, Full name, and Full name + modifier. Such detailed distinction of anaphors is motivated by her basic claim that referring expressions of anaphors can correlate with different degrees of information accessibility.

The idea of Accessibility Theory has been accepted by many researchers in Chinese linguistics, as shown in Y. Xu (2004), Jiang (2004), Weng (2004), and Ding (2005). But few researchers discuss all anaphors as thoroughly as Ariel (1990) does. Using an AT approach, Y. Xu (2004) classifies Chinese anaphoric forms into seven kinds: zero pronoun, reflexives, single demonstratives, pronouns, demonstrative NPs, name, and definite descriptions. Ding (2005) analyzes personal pronouns, noun phrases without definitive[①], and zero pronoun. Shen (2005) is only concerned with bare NPs.

In this thesis, the following five kinds of Chinese anaphoric forms will be taken into account: zero pronouns, the third-person pronoun *ta*, the definite

① The notion of "noun phrase without definitive" in Ding (2005) actually is consistent with the notion of "bare NP".

pronouns *zhe/na*, descriptive NPs in the form of *zhe/na*+NPs, and full NPs.[①] I believe that all major types of Chinese anaphoric forms can be seen as forming a system and they can be regarded as actually marking different degrees of accessibility of the antecedents.

According to the marking relations with the degree of accessibility of the antecedent, those five kinds of Chinese anaphoric forms will be classified into four categories: the zero pronoun, overt pronouns including the third-person pronoun *ta* and the definite pronouns *zhe/na*, descriptive NPs, and full NPs. Since the third-person pronoun *ta* and the definite pronouns *zhe/na* are almost identical in carrying the same descriptive content, they are regarded as the same kind of Chinese anaphoric forms and marking the same degree of accessibility of the antecedent.

In a word, four types of Chinese anaphoric forms in Chinese NP anaphora are identified as the object of study in this thesis: zero pronouns, overt pronouns, descriptive NPs, and full NPs.

## 1.3 Main Proposals of This Thesis

The interpretation of different Chinese anaphoric forms requires an understanding of the interaction between contexts and Chinese anaphoric forms, and different Chinese anaphoric forms are used in different contexts. Then a nature question rises: how do the varying contexts correlate with the use of different anaphoric forms in Chinese discourses?

There are a variety of approaches in the previous research that attempt to account for the interpretation of different Chinese anaphoric forms, including the pragmatic approach, the functional approach, and the semantic approach.

---

① Those five kinds of anaphors are often confused with the same referring expressions. For instance, the zero pronoun has no realized form in the speech flow, which is the same as some empty categories that are resulted from inference and ellipsis. Shen (1994) gives a detailed discussion on all empty categories in Chinese. This thesis will not deal with the referring expressions which are not anaphorically used.

Among the various approaches, it seems that the semantic approach based on the framework of information accessibility is most applicable for the interpretations on Chinese anaphoric forms. If we assume that anaphors always play the same role on people's understanding, no matter how contexts and anaphoric forms vary, we can say that all Chinese anaphoric forms share a common function. On the other hand, there is semantic variability in contexts which require different anaphoric forms. In this respect different Chinese anaphoric forms can be said to differ in specific functions and satisfy different pragmatic requirements. What this implies is that the semantic approach based on information accessibility is fundamental. The difference between Chinese anaphoric forms in the pragmatics or the function actually comes from the semantic variability of different Chinese anaphoric forms.

Thus, this thesis will propose that the mechanisms of the correlation between contexts and anaphoric forms can be revealed when we take into account properties in information accessibility. Although the antecedent and the anaphor may be realized as different referring expressions in discourse information flow, they both denote the same discourse referent. Hence different information expressed by the antecedent and the anaphor respectively can be linked by the same discourse referent, no matter how the antecedent and the anaphor vary in referring expressions. In this respect, there is an accessibility relation between the antecedent and the anaphor in information. Different anaphoric forms are actually resulted from different accessibility relations which vary in the degree of accessibility of the antecedent. So the accessibility of the antecedent is important for the interpretations of different Chinese anaphoric forms.

This thesis suggests that the interpretations on Chinese anaphoric forms should be studied mainly from these two aspects: a) what factors can affect the accessibility of the antecedent, and b) how those factors affect the accessibility of the antecedent.

Four factors are proposed to affect the accessibility of the antecedent: discourse structure, the status of topicality, the saliency in cognition, and referential distance. They are posed to be related with anaphora from two structural aspects: one is the scope of two clauses, and the other is the two discourse entities which occur in two clauses (the antecedent and the anaphor). In terms of the two clauses, they can vary in their relations in discourses and constitute different types of discourse structures which are termed as the super-node structures; while in the domain of the antecedent and the anaphor, they can vary in status as a topical element, with degrees of saliency, and with referential distances.

Three kinds of super-node structures will be distinguished in this thesis: the Minimal Structure (MS), the Local Structure (LS), and the Global Structure (GS). The super-node structures can greatly impact the accessibility of the antecedents. Hence different antecedents in different super-node structures are distinctive in the accessibility. As a result, the super-node structure can distinguish three sets of antecedents with distinct degrees of accessibility. Accordingly a ranking order of antecedents is proposed: Antecedents in the MS > Antecedents in the LS > Antecedents in the GS.

The topicality, the saliency, and referential distance can further affect the accessibility of the antecedents based on the impact of discourse structure. The impacts of those three factors can be revealed by the pairs of the antecedent and the anaphor, in that the pairs of the antecedent and the anaphor can indicate the inference load from the anaphor to the antecedent and the coherence of the discourse. Six distinguished kinds of the pairs of the antecedent and the anaphor are proposed: Strong Continuation, Weak Continuation, Smooth Shift, Rough Shift, Short Link, and Distant Link; which can result in six kinds of distinguished degrees of accessibility of the antecedent. As a result, three sets of antecedents rendered by the super-node structures can be further ranked according to the impacts of those six kinds of the pairs of the antecedent and the anaphor. In other words, topicality, saliency, and referential distance will further rank the available antecedents, illustrated by the above ranking order, of different sets resulted from the impact of discourse structure. Hence another ranking order of antecedents is proposed: Antecedents in Strong Continuation > Antecedents in Weak Continuation > Antecedents in Smooth Shift > Antecedents in Rough Shift > Antecedents in Short Link > Antecedents in Distant Link

Furthermore, the super-node structures based on discourse structure and the ranking order of antecedents based on other three factors can together determine the uses of Chinese anaphoric forms. Firstly, the great impacts of the super-node structures on the accessibility of the antecedent will constraint the uses of possible anaphoric forms in different super-node structures. And secondly the differently ranked antecedents in the ranking order resulted from the AN-pairs will be further correlated with different possible anaphoric forms through the requirement of the inference load from the anaphor to the antecedent.

In general, all the uses of various Chinese anaphoric forms follow the Accessibility Marking Hierarchy: zero pronouns > overt pronouns (the third-person pronoun / the definite pronouns) > descriptive NPs > Full NPs. The marking degree of accessibility of the anaphoric form is higher than that of the anaphoric forms in the hierarchy.

But the general hierarchy can have different representations in different super-node structures, in that the available antecedents and the possible anaphoric forms vary in different super-node structures. In the MS, the most highly accessible antecedents are encoded by the simplest possible anaphoric form- the zero pronoun, the highly accessible antecedents are marked by the simpler possible anaphoric forms- overt pronouns, and the lowly accessible antecedents are marked by the most complex possible anaphoric forms- descriptive NPs. In the LS, the most highly accessible antecedents are also encoded by the simplest possible anaphoric form which is the overt pronoun rather than the zero pronoun according to the constraints of the LS on anaphoric forms, and the highly and lowly accessible antecedents are encoded by descriptive NPs and full NPs respectively. Accordingly, the most highly accessible antecedents in the GS are encoded by descriptive NPs and other antecedents are encoded by full NPs.

## 1.4 Research Methodology and Significances

This thesis will study Chinese anaphoric forms with a theoretical analysis as well as a corpus-based study. Concretely speaking, this thesis will firstly analyze different uses of various kinds of Chinese anaphoric forms and give proposals on the interpretations of Chinese anaphoric forms. I will then take a corpus-based study on the use of all kinds of Chinese anaphoric forms, and then further investigate whether the corpus-based study can support the conceptual analysis. Finally, this thesis will give a general conclusion on the interpretations of Chinese anaphoric forms based on the conceptual analysis and the corpus study.

The research on Chinese anaphoric forms taken by this thesis is expected to make contributions to the universal analysis on the interpretations of anaphoric forms. Besides, I believe that the present research on Chinese anaphoric forms is necessary due to the following considerations. Firstly, further research can help deepen our understanding of Chinese anaphoric forms and consequently provide a better interpretation of the related linguistic phenomena. Secondly, further research can help Chinese teaching in a second language context, enabling learners to be able to tell the difference between different kinds of Chinese anaphoric forms. And thirdly, further research can benefit projects on Chinese anaphor resolutions for information retrieval.

## 1.5 Organization of the Thesis

This thesis is organized as follows.

Chapter 2 will provide an overview on previous research in anaphora. Universal approaches to anaphora as well as the specific research on Chinese anaphora will be discussed.

Chapter 3 will mainly study the interpretations of different Chinese anaphoric forms from the point of view of the information accessibility framework. Two main aspects are considered in the process: what factors will affect the accessibility of the antecedent and the use of Chinese anaphoric forms, and how those factors affect the accessibility of the antecedent and the use of Chinese anaphoric forms. After an in-depth study on those two main aspects, the interpretations of Chinese anaphoric forms can be attempted.

Chapter 4 will conduct a corpus investigation on uses of all Chinese anaphoric forms, and further verify whether the theoretical analysis on the interpretations of Chinese anaphoric forms can be supported by actual data from the corpus.

Chapter 5 will give a brief comparison between the interpretations of this thesis and the previous prominent interpretations on Chinese anaphoric forms.

Chapter 6 will summarize the main research of this thesis and provide the conclusions.

# Chapter 2 Review of the Literature on Anaphora

Anaphora research has been conducted for various languages from different perspectives. This thesis will concentrate on the papers which study English or Chinese anaphora from a discourse perspective, because anaphora is a discourse phenomenon in nature.

## 2.1 English Anaphora Research from a Discourse Perspective

From a discourse perspective, it is believed that anaphora is a main characteristic of connected discourse. Many researchers have made great efforts on discourse anaphora from a diverse range of approaches. Those papers on discourse anaphora in English can be loosely classified into four groups according to the approaches they take: functional approaches, cognitive approaches, semantic approaches, and computational approaches. We will review the major works on English anaphora from those four approaches in turn.

### 2.1.1 Functional Approaches

Halliday and Hasan (1976) propose that cohesion relation is a crucial way to keep a text coherent. They propose four types of cohesion relations: reference, substitution, ellipsis, and conjunction. Halliday and Hasan further sub-classify the reference into four types: Exophora (situational), Endophora (textual), Anaphora (to preceding text), and Cataphora (to following text). The classification on reference provides useful heuristics to the subsequent research.

### 2.1.2 Cognitive Approaches

Unlike generative grammar, which believes that semantics is peripheral, cognitive linguistics assumes that meaning is central to language such that it should be seriously considered and that linguistic structures exist to serve the function of expressing meanings. Accordingly, the research of discourse anaphora from the cognitive approach focuses on what meanings different anaphoric forms can express in discourses. There are two mainstreams on discourse anaphora taking the cognitive approach: Accessibility Theory and Cognitive Grammar, which will be reviewed in subsequent text.

#### 2.1.2.1 Accessibility Theory

The core idea in Accessibility Theory (AT) is that different nominal forms, i.e. different anaphoric forms, can indicate/mark different degrees of accessibility (Cf. Keenan & Comrie (1977), Givón (1983), Ariel (1990, 1994), Gundel et al. (1993), etc.). Hence NP accessibility hierarchies are central to the research, because NP accessibility hierarchies can help to differentiate diverse markers of accessibility. Keenan & Comrie (1977), Givón (1983), Ariel (1990), and Gundel et al. (1993) all propose NP accessibility hierarchies, which will be reviewed below.

**1. Keenan & Comrie (1977)**

Keenan & Comrie (1977) chiefly studies which NPs are accessible for relativization. The relativization process actually refers to the process of a NP being referred back to by an anaphoric form. A NP accessibility hierarchy is established according to the NPs' syntactic positions: Subject > Object > Indirect/oblique object > Genitive > Comparative. If a NP in the accessibility hierarchy is higher, it is more accessible for relativizing in a language and is thus easier to be referred back to by an anaphoric form.

**2. Givón (1983)**

Givón (1983) suggests that all entities are topical to greater or lesser degrees and are referred back to by different anaphoric forms according to their different degrees of accessibility due to different levels of topicality. He further proposes a continuum of degrees of accessibility of topic NPs based on three kinds of measurements: lookback which is to find the distance between the antecedent and the anaphor; ambiguity; and decay according to topic principle. The continuum is represented as follows.

The more continuous/predicate topic

Zero anaphor

Unstressed pronoun

Stressed pronoun

Full NP

Modified full NP

The less continuous/predicate topic

**Fig. 2.1 Givón's Continuum of Topic NPs**

Viewed from the continuum of the degrees of accessibility of topic NPs, the degree of accessibility of a topic is in inverse proportion to its coding material. Specifically, the more accessibility a topic has, the less coding material is used to represent it in language; while the less accessibility a topic has, the more coding material is required.

In other words, Givón correlates the topicality with referring expressions directly. Nevertheless, Givón assumes that the text properties are associated with the cognitive status of entities, such that "What is continuing is more predictable", and "What is predictable is easier to process" (1983:12).

Moreover, Givón focuses on the prediction of the entity being a topic. Centering Theory also concentrates on the prediction of entities, which will be introduced in the succeeding text.

**3. Ariel (1990)**

Ariel's idea is similar to that of Givón. The main difference between them is that Ariel proposes that cognitive status of referents rather than the referring expressions can be characterized in terms of a graded scale.

The basic claim of Ariel's Accessibility Theory is that speakers let hearers know the degree of accessibility of the entity to be retrieved, which is achieved through the choice of referring expressions. She contends that all referring expressions should be viewed as anaphoric in a large context, regardless of whether they do or do not refer, and that referring expressions are linguistically marked to indicate the accessibility of their antecedents. Thus, Ariel's main goal is to find out which degree of accessibility each type of referring expression conventionally encodes.

In Ariel (1990), there are four factors which would play a role in the accessibility of referring expressions.

1) Distance: The distance between the antecedent and the anaphor (recently mentioned entities are more accessible than remotely mentioned ones).

2) Competition: The number of competitors on the role of antecedent (if there is competition of potential antecedents for an anaphoric expression, these antecedents are less accessible than if there is no competition).

3) Saliency: Whether the antecedent is a salient referent or not is mainly determined by many factors: grammatical function, high vs. low physical saliency in the context, order of mention, definiteness and quantification of the DPs.

4) Unity: The antecedent being within vs. without the same frame/ world/point of view/segment or paragraph as the anaphor (the greater degree of cohesion between the clause which contains the antecedent and the clause that contains the anaphor, the greater the accessibility of the anaphor; a conception to include macro-level connectivity between topics, frames, points of view, and so on, and sentence-level degree of connectivity between clauses).

In the actual analyzed process, Ariel mainly makes use of the quantifiable criterion of the above four factors—distance—to determine the accessibility of referring expressions.

Diverse referring expressions will be anaphoric by different anaphoric forms due to their different degrees of accessibility. And various anaphoric forms are consequently considered as the markers of different degrees of accessibility of the antecedent in Ariel (1990), which are called accessibility markers.

Ariel originally distinguishes between three types of accessibility markers:

High, Intermediate, and Low accessibility markers. But subsequently she argues that such a division on accessibility markers is too simple and the degree of accessibility should be a continuum. And then Ariel proposes a detailed Accessibility Marking Scale which includes various types of referring expressions, as indicated below.

High Accessibility Markers

Extremely High Accessibility Markers (gaps)
Cliticized pronoun
Unstressed pronoun
Stressed pronoun
Stressed pronoun + gesture
Proximal demonstrative (+ NP)
Distal demonstrative (+ NP)
Proximal demonstrative + modifier
Distal demonstrative + modifier
First name
Last name
Short definite description
Long definite description
Full ("namy"[①]) name
Full name + modifier

Low Accessibility Markers

**Fig. 2.2 Ariel's Accessibility Marking Scale**

Ariel's Accessibility Marking Scale is not a universal one. But Ariel believes that there are three criteria which could media the association between linguistic forms and degrees of cognitive accessibility in any language: Informativity, Rigidity, and Attenuation. A referring expression is more informative, more rigid and less attenuated, and then the accessibility of the linguistic form is lower.

① Ariel (1990) used the term "namy" to represent full names.

**4. Gundel et al. (1993)**

The observations made in Gundel et al. (1993) are similar to those of Ariel (1990). They all agree that there exists an inverse relation between the specificity of referential expressions and the salience of referents in the context of discourse.

Gundel et al. (1993) differentiate attention statuses for the addressee into six types:

Type identifiable—identify what kinds of thing this is;

Referential—associate a unique representation by the time the sentence is processed;

Uniquely identifiable—associate a unique representation by the time the nominal is processed;

Familiar—associate a representation already in memory;

Activated—associate a representation from working memory;

In focus—associate a representation that your attention is currently focused on.

(Gundel et al. (1993): 275)

Gundel et al. (1993) propose that different forms have different statuses as their conventional meaning, and further put forward a Givenness Hierarchy according to the status:

in focus > activated > familiar > uniquely identifiable > referential > type identifiable

that
[it] this [that N] [ the N] [indefinite this N] [ a N]
this N

**Fig. 2.3 GIVENNESS Hierarchy in Gundel et al. (1993)**

In the Givenness Hierarchy, each status would entail all the statuses to the right on the hierarchy, say a form in focus is consequently activated, familiar, uniquely identifiable, referential, and type identifiable. Conversely, the left status is not specific to the right status, but is not excluded. A form with the left status would have more givenness and be more accessible than a form on the right hand side.

### 2.1.2.2 Cognitive Grammar on Anaphora

Cognitive Grammar is developed by Langacker (1987, 1988, 1991, and 1993). Van Hoek (1992, 1995a, 1995b, 1997, 2003) establishes a model of anaphora based on Langacker's reference point.

**1. Langacker**

In Cognitive Grammar (CG), Langacker proposes that language is made of three units: semantic, symbolic and phonological unit. "Grammar is itself symbolic" and is "the pairing of a semantic structure and a phonological structure" (Langacker (2008)).

In Langacker's Cognitive Grammar, a pair of notions is important: a reference point and dominion. Langacker (1991) proposes a reference point / dominion configuration to deal with the relationship of possessor and possessum. A possessor functions as a reference point through which one can make mental contact with the possessum. The notion "a reference point" in CG is similar to Chafe's (1994) notion of a "starting point".

Langacker (1996, 2000, 2001, 2002, and 2008) argue that his CG is capable of interpreting language phenomena in discourses. And Langacker (2000, 2001, and 2002) put forward the idea of Current Discourse Space (CDS) to account for discourse anaphora.

*Current Discourse Space (CDS) is a mental space, which consists of elements and relation construed as being shared by the speaker and the addressee as a basis for communication at a given moment in the flow of discourse.*

*Langacker 2000: 262*

CDS will be updated by the "input" CDS. Various referring expressions have different implications to CDS. The indefinite nominal element implies that no unique instance of the type in question is yet accessible in the CDS. A definite nominal element implies that a unique instance of the specified type is indeed accessible in the CDS. A pronoun implies that its referent is not only accessible in the CDS, but also has already been singled out.

**2. Van Hoek**

Van Hoek develops Langacker's reference point / dominion configuration into a Reference Point Model to explain intra-sentential pronominal anaphora. And she also merges the idea of AT into her Reference Point Model.

Van Hoek proposes that the context can be defined in terms of conceptual reference point. A reference point is a conception that is prominent and therefore is used as a starting point from which to apprehend a larger conception of which it is part. The dominion of a referent point consists of the elements that are conceptually located relative to the reference point, whose construal is shaped by their association with the reference point. Within a sentence, the reference point functions as "local topic". And there may be a sequence of reference points, each within the dominion of preceding reference points.

Van Hoek posits that the organization of reference points is determined primarily by prominence and semantic connectivity, and is also affected by linear word order and point of view to a lesser extent.

The prominence of a nominal depends on its position in a sentence according to Keenan and Comrie's (1977) NP Accessibility Hierarchy: Subject > Direct Object > Oblique. In a sentence, the subject is the most prominent, and it is thus the first reference point. The direct object accordingly functions as a second reference point due to its less prominence in contrast with the subject.

A prominent nominal tends to be construed as a reference point in relation to elements with which it is directly interconnected. The connectivity between different elements belongs to semantic connectivity. Actually semantic connectivity is a conceptual connectivity. Connectivity is determined primarily by interconnecting relations such as process relations in which both reference point and nominal element are complements. Conceptual connectivity is a continuum. Van Hoek (2003:186) divides it into three types: 1) **Tight Connectivity**: Elements are bound together so tightly that there is no flexibility in construal; 2) **Loose Connectivity**: Elements are interconnected a bit more loosely, so that some speakers might construe the name as being outside the dominion of the pronoun and therefore acceptable, though other speakers might not; and 3) **Non-Connectivity**: Elements are interrelated so loosely that many speakers prefer that the referent be re-established with a name, as the original reference point seems a bit distant to continue reference via a pronoun.

As to linear word order, a nominal encountered earlier in the sentence tends to be construed as a reference point relative to nominal elements encountered later.

### 2.1.3 Anaphora Research with a Semantic Approach

The semantic approach to anaphora tries to find out semantic variability of different anaphoric forms. The main research including Discourse Representation Theory (DRT) and Modal Subordination will be reviewed in subsequent text.

**1. Discourse Representation Theory (DRT)**

Discourse Representation Theory (DRT) is a theory of dynamic interpretations of natural language proposed by Hans Kamp. The basic idea of DRT is that a natural language discourse (a sequence of sentences uttered by the same speaker) is interpreted in the context of a representation structure. The result of the processing of a piece of discourse in the context of representation structure R is a new representation structure R′; the new structure R′ can be viewed as an updated version of R.

Formally, a discourse representation structure R consists of two parts: a finite list of discourse referents, and a finite list of conditions. The discourse referents in the list are called the discourse referents of R. The conditions of a structure R may contain discourse referents that are not included in the list of discourse referents of R. Conditions can be atoms, links, or complex conditions. An atom is a predicate name applied to a number of discourse referents, a link is an expression $t = r$, where r is a discourse referent, and t is either a proper name or a discourse referent. The clause for complex conditions uses recursion: a complex condition is a condition of the form $R \Rightarrow R'$, where R and R′ are discourse representation structures (DRS).

Kamp (1981) and Kamp & Reyle (1990) impose formal constraints on the availability of discourse referents for anaphoric linking based on DRS. Roughly, the set of available discourse referents consists of the discourse referents of the current structure, plus the discourse referents of structures that can be reached from the current one by a series of steps in the directions *left*, i.e. from the consequent of a pair $R \Rightarrow R'$ to the antecedent, and *up*, i.e. from a structure to an encompassing structure. The constraints on the accessibility of discourse referents are used to explain the awkwardness of anaphoric links as in (2.1).

(2.1)*If every man$_1$ meets an attractive woman$_2$, he$_1$ smiles at her$_2$.

The discourse representation structure for the example (2.1) is shown below.

(2.2)

```
u  v
-------------------------
| x y                   |
|-----------------------|
| man (x)               |
| an attractive woman (y)|
-------------------------
meet (x, y)
u=x
v=y
smile (u,v)
```

In (2.1), the entity *every man* and *an attractive woman* are encoded by the overt pronouns *he* and *her* respectively when they are referred back to in succeeding clause. But the example is infelicitous. The main reason of the infelicity in (2.1), according to DRT, is that the DRS the anaphor occurs is beyond the DRS its antecedent occurs, which violates the accessibility condition in DRT.

In all, the life span of a discourse referent depends on the way in which it was introduced. All "alive" referents may serve as antecedents for anaphors in subsequent discourse. Anaphoric pronouns are represented as free variables linked to appropriate antecedent variables. Definite descriptions in their simplest use are treated in a way which is similar to the treatment of anaphoric pronouns; while definite noun phrases in their anaphoric use are treated like indefinite noun phrases, i.e. they are translated as free variables, but give rise to additional anaphoric links. The difference between indefinite noun phrases and definite noun phrases / pronouns is that, indefinites introduce new variables, whereas the variables introduced by definites and pronouns always are linked to an already established context. Discourse referents for proper names are always available for anaphoric reference, and are always included in the list of discourse referents of the top level structure.

**2. Modal Subordination**

Roberts (1986, 1989, 1990, 1996) examine modal subordination in detail.

Modal subordination is a phenomenon which stems from the relationship between propositions in a discourse. Look at two examples from Roberts (1989):

(2.3)a. If John bought a book, he'll be home reading it by now.

b. * It's a murder mystery.

(2.4)a. If John bought a book, he'll be home reading it by now.

b. It'll be a murder mystery.

Both examples (2.3 & 2.4) are considered "donkey sentences". The indefinite NP *a book* serves as the antecedent for a pronoun outside its scope. The example (2.3) is infelicitous, while the syntactically similar example (2.4) is felicitous.

Roberts calls the phenomenon in examples (2.3 & 2.4) modal subordination. Modal subordination is not constrained within anaphora phenomenon in "donkey sentences". It is a phenomenon in which the interpretation of a clause α is taken to involve a modal operator whose force is relativized to some set β of contextually given propositions. And it would say that in that context, α is interpreted as modally subordinate to the propositions in β, or, that α is modally subordinate to the clauses used to express β. Intrasententially, the consequence of a conditional is modally subordinate to the antecedent clause, as in conditional donkey sentences. Intersententially, modal subordination involves the accommodation of material from prior utterances to serve the role of an antecedent for the subordinate clause. In both cases, the antecedent clause plays a crucial part in determining the derived context set which is used to restrict the range of the operator over the modally subordinate clause. And in cases which involved pronominal anaphora, the accommodation is constrained by the requirement of explicit prior representation of potential anaphoric antecedents.

### 2.1.4 Computational Approaches

The computational approach to discourse anaphora is to provide an algorithm for computer to find out the right antecedent for an anaphor. Two influential theories underlying the computational approach will be reviewed in this part: Centering Theory (CT) and COT which is developed based on CT.

**1. Centering Theory**

The terminology Centering Theory (CT) firstly appears in Grosz, Joshi, and Weinstein (1983) (GJW83). Grosz, Joshi, and Weinstein (1986 and 1995) continue to give detailed descriptions on the centering framework and the theory proposed in GJW83. After GJW95, CT have attracted much attention and been widely studied (e.g. Byron (1998), Walker (1998), Poesio et al. (2000), Forbes (2002)).

CT concerns itself with relationships among focus of attention, choice of referring expression, and perceived coherence of utterances within a discourse segment. It results from the fusion of two lines of thought. One is the ideas from Grosz and Sidner's work on anaphora resolution and discourse coherence, the work which has appeared in their models of local and global discourse structure (Grosz (1977), Sidner (1983), Grosz and Sidner (1986)). The other is the work on inference in discourse by Joshi and associates (Joshi and Kuhn (1979), Joshi and Weinstein (1981)).

CT uses the term *centers* of an utterance to refer to those entities serving to link that utterance to other utterances in the discourse segment that contains it. Centers are semantic objects, not words, phrases, or syntactic forms.

Each utterance U in a discourse segment (DS) is assigned a set of *forward-looking centers,* $C_f(U)$; each utterance other than the segment initial utterance is assigned a single *backward-looking center,* $C_b(U)$.

For a discourse segment made of by $U_1$, …, $U_t$, there are some constraints on $C_f(U_n)$ and $C_b(U_n)$.

① There are a set of $C_f$s in an utterance. But there is only one $C_b$.

For $U_n$, $C_f(U_n)=\{e_1,e_2,e_3,\ldots,e_p\}$

For $U_n$, $C_b(U_n)=\{$ utterance $e_x$ or undefined$\}$

② $C_f$ should be realized partially in the next utterance.

③ The elements of $C_f$ in an utterance are partially ordered to reflect relative prominence, which is the rank of $C_f$.

④ The backward-looking center of utterance $U_{n+1}$ ($C_b(U_{n+1})$) connects with one of the forward-looking centers of utterance $U_n$ ($C_f(U_n)$). Moreover, The more highly ranked an element of $C_f(U_n)$, the more likely it is to be $C_b(U_{n+1})$. The most highly ranked element of $C_f$ ($U_n$) that is realized in $U_{n+1}$ is the $C_b(U_{n+1})$.

For $U_n$: $C_b$ ($U_n$)=a, $C_f(U_n)=(e_1,e_2,...,e_p)$, a=$e_k$, for some k.

For $U_{n+1}$: $C_b(U_{n+1})$ realizes $e_m$ and, for all j, j<m, $e_j$ is not realized in $U_{n+1}$; i.e. $e_m$ is realized in $U_{n+1}$ and no higher ranked $e_j$ is realized in $U_{n+1}$.

The ranking of $C_f$ in an utterance is determined by their grammatical role: SUBJECT > OBJECT(S) > OTHER.

Based on the different relations between $C_b$ and $C_f$ across pairs of utterances, CT defines four types of transition states, which are shown in the table below.

**TABLE 2.1 Transition States in Centering Theory**

| | $C_b(U_n)=C_b(U_{n-1})$ or $C_b(U_{n-1})$ undefined | $C_b(U_n)\neq C_b(U_{n-1})$ |
|---|---|---|
| $C_b(U_n)=C_p(U_n)$ | Continue | Smooth Shift |
| $C_b(U_n)\neq C_p(U_n)$ | Retain | Rough Shift |

Furthermore, CT posits are two important rules in CT which are given below.

Rule 1: If any element of $C_f(U_n)$ is realized by a pronoun in $U_{n-1}$, then the $C_b(U_{n+1})$ must also be realized by a pronoun.

Rule 2: *Sequences* of continuation are preferred over *sequences* of retaining; and sequences of retaining are to be preferred over sequences of shifting.

Rule 1 is the basic constraint on center realization of referring expressions, which stipulates that no element in an utterance can be realized as a pronoun unless the backward-looking center of the utterance is also realized as a pronoun. In this rule, one function of pronominal reference is represented: the use of a pronoun to realize the Cb signals the hearer that the speaker is continuing to talk about the same thing. But Rule 1 does not preclude using pronouns for other entities so long as the Cb is realized with a pronoun.

Rule 2 is the basic constraint on center movement, which indicates a preference rank of transition state: Continue > Retain > Smooth Shift > Rough Shift. Rule 2 reflects that transition states affect the coherence of a segment. In a locally coherent discoursc segment, shifts are followed by a sequence of continuations characterizing another stretch of locally coherent discourse.

Frequent shifting leads to a lack of local coherence. They should plan ahead to minimize the number of shifts. This rule predicts that certain sequences produce a higher inference load than others.

**2. Centering Model Based on Optimality Theory (COT)**

The main ideas of CT have been accepted and used as a basis of a new theory by many researchers. For example, Walker (1998) extends CT to the global discourse structure, which is called Cache Model. Cristea et al. (1998) integrates Rhetorical Structure Theory into the CT. Tetreault (2000) takes a corpus-based evaluation on CT from the computational perspective. COT is also one of the extended theories based on CT.

Beaver (2004) reformulates the Centering model of anaphora resolution and discourse coherence (Grosz, Joshi and Weistein (1995)) in terms of Optimality Theory (OT) (Prince and Smolensky (1993)).

First, he makes a terminology change: he uses *topic* instead of *backward-looking center*. The definition of *topic* is as follows.

*The topic of a sentence is the entity referred to in both the current and the previous sentence, such that the relevant referring expression in the previous sentence was minimally oblique. If there is no such entity, the topic is undefined.*

*Beaver 2004: 12*

Second, Beaver provides six constraints and the rank order of those constraints outline below.

*AGREE Anaphoric expressions agree with their antecedents in terms of number and gender.*

*DISJOINT Co-arguments of a predicate are disjoint.*

*PRO-TOP The topic is pronominalized.*

*FAM-DEF Each definite NP is familiar. This means both that the referent is familiar, and that no new information about the referent is provided by the definite.*

*COHERE The topic of the current sentence is the topic of the previous one.*

*ALIGN The topic is in subject position.*

*Beaver 2004: 13*

The above six constraints can be ranked with an order in which the top constraint is the highest ranked. The top two constraints, AGREE and DISJOINT reflect ideas that are familiar from the syntactic literature, the second mirroring the effect of Principle B from the Binding Theory.① PRO-TOP has essentially reflected the effect of CT's Rule 1. However, in COT constraints are defeasible. PRO-TOP will function comparably to Rule 1 if there are pronouns in an utterance. But if there are no pronouns, then all candidate interpretations will be equally bad as far as PRO-TOP is concerned. But the interaction of PRO-TOP and the lower ranked FAM-DEF produces the effect of Rule 1's indefeasibility. It should be noted that the class of definites governed by FAMDEF is taken to include pronouns, definite descriptions and proper names. The last two constraints, COHERE and ALIGN are just the conditions used in BFP to specify transition types.

Here is an example in Beaver (2004).

(2.5) a. Jane$_i$ likes Mary$_j$ .

b. She$_k$ often visits her$_l$ for tea$_m$.

c. The woman$_n$ is a compulsive tea drinker.

Since there is no previous sentence, the topic of (2.5a) is undefined by definition. For the second sentence (2.5b), it is constructed by a table.

**TABLE 2.2 COT on the Example (2.5b)**

| Example (2.5b) | AGREE | DISJOINT | PRO-TOP | FAM-DEF | COHERE | ALIGN |
|---|---|---|---|---|---|---|
| ☆ k=i, l=j | | | | | * | |
| k=l=i | | * | | | * | |
| k=j, l=i | | | | | * | * |
| k=l=j | | * | | | * | |
| k=i, l∉{i,j} | | | | * | * | |
| k=j, l∉{i,j} | | | | * | * | |
| k∉{i,j}, l=i | | | | * | * | * |
| k∉{i,j}, l=j | | | | * | * | * |
| k, l∉{i,j}, k≠l | | | * | ** | * | * |
| k=l∉{i,j} | | * | * | ** | * | * |

① Principle B typically differs from DISJOINT. Principle B is stated as: Pronouns are locally free.

In the above table, the top row lists the input example (2.5b), and then the constraints in rank order, with the strongest constraints on the left. Each of the following rows details the behavior of one candidate interpretation with respect to the constraints, each asterisk marking a constraint violation. The best of the candidates under consideration is found by looking at each constraint column from the left until finding a column in which one candidate has fewer violations than any other. This is then the optimal candidate, and is signaled with a "☆".

According to Table 2.2, the optimal candidate of (2.5b) is the first one "k=i, l=j", which only violates one lower constraint "COHERE". That is, "she" takes "Jane" as its antecedent, and "her" takes "Mary" as its antecedent, which is consistent with our intuition.

Now it is time to consider resolution possibilities for the definite NP "The woman$_n$" in example (2.5c).

**Table 2.3　COT on the Example (2.5c)**

| Example (2.5c) | AGREE | DISJOINT | PRO-TOP | FAM-DEF | COHERE | ALIGN |
|---|---|---|---|---|---|---|
| ☆n=k | | | * | | | |
| n=l | | | * | | * | |
| n=m | | | * | * | * | |
| n∉ {k,l,m} | | | * | * | * | * |

According to Table 2.3, PRO-TOP fails for all candidate interpretations, so this constraint cannot affect resolution in example (2.5c). The candidate interpretation "n=k" only violates one constraint: PRO-TOP, which arouses the least violation by contrast with other three candidate interpretations. Thus the interpretation "n=k" is the optimal interpretation based on COT in which the definite NP "The woman$_n$" chooses "she$_k$" as its antecedent.

Moreover, Beaver states that COT is equally suited for generation or interpretation, comparing that CT and BFP algorithm are suited for interpretation only.

### 2.1.5 Topicality / Saliency / Discourse Structure / Accessibility and Anaphoric Forms

We have examined major research on English anaphora with functional, cognitive, semantic, and computational approaches. There are a variety of theories among them on the interpretations of different anaphoric forms in English. In fact they all attempt to explain uses of different anaphoric forms from the perspective of the topicality, the saliency① in cognitive psychology, discourse structure, with some of them using accessibility as a general term to cover the topicality, saliency and discourse structure.

Different theories result in different factors identified and different analysis and different conclusions provided. The functional approach to anaphora research assumes that language is a communicative system and that discourse anaphora is viewed as an important cohesive way to communicate. Hence it tries to explain which kind of anaphoric forms can provide enough cohesive requirements for a communicative context. The cognitive approach to anaphora research believes that discourse anaphora has a special meaning in mental representation and different anaphoric forms have different cognitive status to the reader. The semantic approach argues that semantic variability of different anaphoric forms is fundamental for their uses. And the computational approach seeks to establish a computational model which can differentiate different uses of different anaphoric forms in terms of some algorithm.

But all theories make use of the notions of topicality, the saliency, discourse structure, or accessibility. Concretely speaking, topicality, the saliency, discourse structure, and referential distance are widely believed to be correlated with the uses of different anaphoric forms. And the notion of accessibility integrates them into a whole. It can be indicated that the general term "accessibility" can contribute to a more comprehensive analysis on the uses of anaphoric forms.

Besides, most of the theories discussed above on the basis of discourse anaphora in English are declared to be universal. Hence many of them have been

① The term "saliency" is the same with the term "the salience" in literatures. They both refer to the status of the entities in cognitive psychology.

applied to interpret uses of different Chinese anaphoric forms.

## 2.2 Chinese Anaphora Research from a Discourse Perspective

Discourse anaphora is also one of the hot research topics in Chinese linguistics. As early as the 1970s, Li and Thompson (1978) analyze one salient anaphora—zero anaphora—in Modern Chinese. Discourse anaphora attracts more and more researchers thereafter, especially after the 1990s. And the research on discourse anaphora in Chinese consequently thrives with numerous studies. Our review will focus on those studies on Chinese following the neo-Gricean, functional, AT, CG, or CT approaches.

### 2.2.1 Anaphora Research with a Neo-Gricean Approach

#### 2.2.1.1 Overview on Neo-Gricean Approach

Huang (1994) proposes a pragmatic theory of Chinese anaphora within the neo-Gricean framework of conversational implicature. In that paper, Chinese anaphora resolution is largely based on "the systematic interaction of two neo-Gricean pragmatic principles, namely the M[anner]-and I[nformativeness]-principles (in that order of priority), constrained by a Disjoint Reference Presumption (DRP), information saliency and general consistency conditions on conversational implicature".

Huang (1994) argues that pragmatic factors are fundamental to Chinese anaphora. Syntax and pragmatics are interconnected to determine many of the processes of anaphora. What pragmatics does is to provide a set of complementary, explanatory principles which constraints the interpretation or production of an utterance whose linguistic representation has already been antecedently cognized.

#### 2.2.1.2 Evaluations

I believe anaphora is rooted in the linguistic mechanism rather than pragmatic motivation. Hence the Neo-Gricean approach is not appropriate to be used to interpret Chinese anaphoric forms, in my opinion.

## 2.2.2 Anaphora Research with a Functional Approach

### 2.2.2.1 Overview

In the early stage of discourse anaphora research in Chinese, most research is carried out with the functional approach, such as Q. Liao (1986) and P. Chen (1987). Some later projects in M. Pu (1998) and J. Xu (2002 and 2003) also analyze Chinese anaphora from a functional approach.

Q. Liao is a famous forerunner of Chinese anaphora research taking a discourse perspective. He examines a large number of examples of Chinese anaphora and tries to find out the hidden regularity behind those phenomena, which has greatly enlightened the following research on Chinese anaphora.

Chen (1987) analyzes constraints on zero anaphora based on Chinese discourse structure. Discourse structure includes two aspects: micro-continuity and macro-continuity. Micro-continuity refers to the positions of the antecedent and the anaphor in the sentence containing them. Macro-continuity refers to relations between sentences containing the antecedent and the anaphor in discourse structure.

Pu (1998) examines the following factors determining the occurrence and distribution of zero anaphora in Chinese: cognitive constraints, discourse context, pragmatic and semantic information, and speaker/writer-audience interaction.

J. Xu has many publications on Chinese discourse anaphora. His book Xu (2003) and his dissertation J. Xu (2002) will be reviewed in this thesis. Xu (2002) is mainly concerned with the noun-anaphora in Chinese, and Xu (2003) analyzes all three types of anaphora in Chinese: zero anaphora, pronoun anaphora and noun anaphora.

Before analyzing Chinese anaphora, Xu proposes two notions: discourse clause（篇章小句） and Discourse Anaphoric Chain（篇章回指链）. Discourse Anaphoric Chain is a concept designed to describe how an entity is anaphoric in discourse information flow. Discourse Anaphoric Chain can be exprcssed by the notion "node".

Based on those two notions Xu further discusses the phenomenon of zero anaphor in Chinese. He concentrates on zero anaphora in Chinese "multi-verb sentences". And Xu suggests that constraints for zero anaphora in sentences are mainly realized as referential distance and lexical meaning. He also points out that contextual and pragmatic factors are important for zero anaphora resolution.

In the study of pronoun anaphora in Chinese, the third-person pronoun *ta* is extensively analyzed. Xu examines the third-person pronoun *ta* from the linear and hierarchical perspective. Viewed from the linear perspective, *ta* mostly takes the subject, object, and the attribute positions. The degree hierarchy of topic continuity proposed is: zero anaphor > *ta* > noun phrase. Viewed from the hierarchical perspective, the amount of discourse clauses which *ta* can control is less than that which NP can control. Moreover, discourse structure and pragmatic factors also can affect the distribution of pronoun.

As to noun-anaphora, Xu proposes that noun-anaphora can be divided into five types: identical repetition, partial repetition, apposition, superordinate/hyponymy and figurative/metaphorical usages. Those five types of noun-anaphora have different distributions and contribute to the construction of an ideational instantial knowledge system which can explain the uses of different noun-anaphors.

Moreover, those five types of noun-anaphora may be ranked in the following order according to the frequency of occurrence: identical repetition → apposition → partial repetition → superordinate/hyponymy → figurative/metaphorical usages. Xu further discusses why certain types occur more frequently and gives some constraints on their usage.

There are three potential slots including the subject, object, and adjunct/prepositional phrase for a noun-anaphor to occur in a clause. Xu (2002) investigates the distribution of each type of noun-anaphora in those three slots. Xu reveals how each type of noun-anaphora is distributed in the head slot or in the modifier slot through comprehensive analysis. As to their distributions as Theme or Rheme, Xu shows how noun-anaphors tend to occur in the theme instead of Rheme, and explains this phenomenon with reference to Halliday's (1994) discussion of theme-rheme structure.

Xu also applies Matthiessen's (1995) notion of ideational instantial knowledge system to analyze noun-anaphora in Chinese texts. The hypothesis of Matthiessen is that the text is organized by spans, hierarchically organized from the smallest at clause level up to the text as a whole. The relations between spans are described in rhetorical structure theory. The occurrence of noun-anaphors in a text is conditioned not only by the linear order of grammatical units, but also by their hierarchical structure.

**2.2.2.2 Evaluations**

It can be indicated from the above review that the functional approach to anaphora research in Chinese is chiefly to apply RST to analyze Chinese anaphora.

RST is a theory about discourse structure, rather than a theory about anaphora. It chiefly proposes that there are a number of rhetorical relations which hold between different units of a text and rhetorical relations are recursively applied to spans of text until all spans are part of a rhetorical relation.

Some previous research argues that the discourse structure plays an important role in the interpretations on Chinese anaphoric forms (Cf. Chen (1987), J. Xu (2002 and 2004), D. Wang (2006), etc.). The application of RST in Chinese anaphora research is to foreground the important factor of discourse structure. For instance, J. Xu (2002 and 2004) applies RST to interpret different uses of Chinese anaphoric forms. But there are three main problems in the application of RST on interpreting the uses of Chinese anaphoric forms.

Firstly, rhetorical relations are difficult to define. Rhetorical relations are defined on the basis of various semantic connections. But sometimes semantic difference between two connections is subtle. And it will thus be difficult to distinguish them.

Secondly, it is difficult to determine how many rhetorical relations are needed on the interpretations of Chinese anaphoric forms.

There is a variety of rhetorical relations in literatures. Mann and Thompson (1988) define 24 classical rhetorical relations, and six more relations have been added more recently to produce a total of 30 extended RST relations. SDRT has mentioned many rhetorical relations. And RST and SDRT both propose that the set of rhetorical relations is open-ended. Moreover, there have been a number of efforts to develop alternate collections of relations which are distinct from the rhetorical relations in RST and founded on some alternate basis. For instance, Hovy and Maier (Hovy and Maier (1995); Maier and Hovy (1991, 1993)) propose to use language metafunctions (ideational, interpersonal, textual), to arrive at a total of about 70 relations, applied to text generation (Hovy et al. (1992)). A similar approach is the use of Halliday's (1985) classification of relations among clauses into elaboration, enhancement and extension (Maier and Hovy (1993)). This work is based on a large collection of about 350 relations from various sources (Hovy (1990)). Grosz and Sidner (1986) propose that two relations (dominance and satisfaction-precedence) are sufficient to characterize discourse structure. For a summary of these and other proposals, see Nicholas (1994).

It can be revealed that there are some controversies either in the types of rhetorical relations or in the definitions of different rhetorical relations. The trickier one is how many rhetorical relations should be needed in the interpretations of Chinese anaphoric forms, which is very difficult to determine. Chen (1987) and J. Xu (2002 and 2004) all have not mentioned the above problem. But it is inevitable for the interpretations of Chinese anaphoric forms based on rhetorical relations.

Thirdly, it is difficult to fully interpret different uses of Chinese anaphoric forms only with RST.

RST is only concerned with the semantic relation between different clauses or units rather than the relation between the antecedent and the topic. As is well known, the antecedent and the anaphor will affect the uses of Chinese anaphoric forms, such as their positions in a clause. But RST cannot reveal the effect of the antecedent and the anaphor on uses of Chinese anaphoric forms, and it consequently cannot well interpret different uses of Chinese anaphoric forms. J. Xu (2002) has noticed that problem and posed some other factors besides rhetorical relations to interpret the uses of Chinese anaphoric forms, say referential distance. But the roles of some other factors have not been fully revealed, and hence different uses of Chinese anaphoric forms still cannot be interpreted clearly.

To sum up, RST cannot rightly interpret different uses of Chinese anaphoric forms.

### 2.2.3 Accessibility Theory

#### 2.2.3.1 Overview

Accessibility Theory has inspired discourse anaphora research in Chinese, such as Y. Xu (2002, 2003, 2004, and 2005), Jiang (2004), Ding (2005), Zhang (2005), and so on. Y. Xu (2002, 2003, 2004, and 2005) concentrates on Chinese anaphora based on Accessibility Theory. Jiang (2004) focuses on the research of zero anaphora in Chinese by applying Accessibility Theory. Ding (2005) studies the accessibility of personal pronouns, noun phrases without definitives, and zero pronouns in Chinese discourse anaphora processing. Y. Xu (2000) and Zhang (2005) compare accessibility markers between Chinese and English in different styles. Y. Xu (2002, 2003, 2004, and 2005), Jiang (2004), and Ding (2005) will be mainly examined in this part.

**1. Y. Xu (2002, 2003, 2004, and 2005)**

Xu proposes that there are two factors which are important for the decoding of anaphora in Mandarin Chinese. One is the topicality of the antecedent; the other is the accessibility of the anaphor.

The topicality of the antecedent means whether an antecedent is in the topic position or not, which could be determined through actual context.

Chinese anaphors are classified into three categories according to the marking accessibility: high, intermediate, and low accessibility markers. Chinese zero anaphors, reflexives, and single demonstratives generally are high accessibility markers, signaling that their referents are easily accessible. Pronouns and demonstrative NP are intermediate accessibility markers, signaling that it is relatively difficult to access their referents in contrast with high accessibility markers. Name and definite descriptions are usually low accessibility markers, signaling that their referents are very difficult to access.

Xu proposes that the interaction between the topicality of the antecedent and the accessibility of the anaphors can explain most of anaphora in Chinese.

A notion "Expected Topic" is an important term in Xu's analysis on anaphora resolution in Chinese. An Expected Topic is defined as a referring expression that is most likely to continue as a topic. Xu (2005) proposes that an NP introduced by an existential/representative sentence is the most typical Expected Topic. According to Xu, if an entity is mentioned as an expected topic, the referent remains in the mind of the hearer. As the processing of a discourse goes on further, there will be more unused/unrealized expected topics that are supposed to be stored in the form of a stack, called a Topic Stack. A freshly introduced expected topic will be kept on the top of all the previously introduced ones in the stack. The one on the very top of a stack is easiest to retrieve. The deeper the expected topic is in the stack, the harder it is to be retrieved.

How deep an expected topic is will affect the choice of anaphoric form to represent it. A low accessibility marker has to be used to retrieve an unused expected topic when it lies deep in the Topic Stack. Conversely, a higher accessibility marker can be used to retrieve an expected topic which is stored near the top of the Topic Stack.

Thus, an ***Anaphora Interpretation Principle*** is proposed: a High Accessibility Marker refers to either the Topic of the clause or a salient Expected Co-Topic in the foregoing clause; an Intermediate Accessibility Marker refers to the first member of the Expected Topic Stack or the Expected Co-Topic; and a Low Accessibility Marker is used to clarify a discourse entity, to indicate a topic shift, or to re-identify a long displaced topic, or a shift of scene or activity with the current topic.

**2. Jiang (2004)**

Jiang (2004) mainly studies syntactic and discourse features of zero anaphora in Chinese, and then provides a zero anaphora resolution.

Based on Y. Xu's anaphora interpretation model which is established on the basis of an interaction between the topicality of the antecedent and the accessibility expressed by the anaphors, Jiang (2004) proposes that the degree of topicality and accessibility of the related referents could be further sub-classified in terms of the different syntactic positions they adopt and the semantic structural hierarchy of the clauses in which they occur.

By analyzing the syntactic positions of both the antecedent and the zero anaphor, Jiang (2004) establishes a hierarchy of the co-referential relations of the syntactic positions of both the antecedent and the zero anaphor as follows: T-T/S/O>S-T/S>SM-SM>O-O>SM-S>S-SM>O-T/S>S-O>OM-S>OBL-O>SM-O.

Viewed from the above hierarchy, referential positions of the antecedent and the anaphor are either the same or shifted. Jiang (2004) proposes that discourse structure can account for the behavior of referential position of the antecedent and the anaphor, in which the shifts mostly occur in the discourse structure where the hierarchical structure is also observed, or the maintenance of referential positions usually occurs in conjoining structures.

Long distance zero anaphora is also a concerned issue in Jiang (2004). It is argued that there are two discourse structures in which long distance reference could take place: 1) the structure in which there is intervening lower-level clause/sentence; and 2) the structure in which two levels of parallel clauses are involved. Moreover, it is found that the co-referential NPs usually occur in parallel positions in long distance zero co-reference.

Finally, Jiang (2004) proposes two principles for zero anaphora interpretation in Chinese text: 1) ZA Interpretation Principle Based on Syntactic Positions, and 2) ZA Interpretation Principle Based on Structural Hierarchy. Jiang indicates that the right interpretation rate of zero anaphora in his Chinese data could reach 89.3% with applying the first principle and further reach 97.1% with applying two principles.

**3. Ding (2005)**

Ding (2005) studies the accessibility of personal pronouns, noun phrases without definitives, and zero pronouns in Chinese discourse anaphora processing.

He claims that in Chinese discourses zero pronouns express the pragmatic meaning of modesty rather than make discourse coherent for its higher accessibility than personal pronouns, especially in the form of the first person; and that noun phrases without definitives in Chinese discourses tend to be interpreted as non-definitives and its anaphora processing is influenced by meaning of verbs and discourse context.

#### 2.2.3.2 Limitations of Accessibility Theory

AT seems a useful approach to interpret Chinese anaphoric forms, but there are some limitations in it.

First, the factors to determine the degree of accessibility of the antecedent has not been thoroughly considered in AT.

In Ariel (1990), one of the foundational works of AT, 'accessibility' is defined as a general term which encompasses the notions of distance, competition, saliency, and unity. Every nominal in a discourse is said to have some degrees of accessibility according to the distance, the competition, the saliency, and the unity.

But in the actual analysis, only the distance is taken to be the main factor which determines the degree of accessibility of the antecedent. So how other three factors affect the accessibility of the antecedent has not been achieved in AT.

Second, it is hard to differentiate different degrees of accessibility of various nominals according to the factors of distance, competition, saliency, and unity.

As mentioned above, "accessibility" is a general term which includes four aspects: the distance, the competition, the saliency, and the unity. Those four aspects play equal roles on the determination of the degree of accessibility. Since there are a lot of compositions of those four aspects, they will render a number of degrees of accessibility. For instance, different distances or different saliency will result in different degrees of accessibility. But as the compositions of those four aspects are general but not exact, it is very difficult to determine the degree of accessibility precisely. For example, assuming two aspects—competition and unity—are the same and the other two aspects—distance and saliency—are different, one is short distance and low salience, and the other is long distance and high salience. Which one has the higher degree of accessibility? It is not easy to tell.

Third, the gap between the degree of accessibility of the antecedent and anaphoric forms has not been interpreted in AT.

Ariel proposes that there is the mediation between linguistic forms (anaphoric forms) and degrees of accessibility (the nominals being anaphoric) according to three criterions: Informativity, Rigidity, and Attenuation. A referring expression is more informative, more rigid (unambiguous) and less attenuated (longer or louder but with no added information), then the accessibility of the linguistic form is lower.

The mediation between the antecedent and the anaphor is actually a gap in AT. There are infinite degrees of accessibility of nominals, whereas anaphoric forms are finite. Hence how to determine the anaphoric form as to some degree of accessibility of a nominal? For example,

(2.6) a. A plane crashed yesterday in New York. This plane flew everyday from Miami to New York.

b. ? A plane crashed yesterday in New York. The plane flew everyday from Miami to New York.

In the above example (2.6), the nominal *a plane* should have the same degree of accessibility either in (2.6a) or (2.6b). But it is preferred to choose *this plane* rather than *the plane* to be the anaphoric form of the nominal *a plane*. We cannot help asking why to choose *this plane* rather than *the plane* to refer back such degree of accessibility of the nominal. The answer cannot be obtained according to the mediation of AT.

Fourth, it is hard to differentiate various Chinese anaphoric forms according to AT.

According to the classification based on AT, different anaphoric forms can mark the same degree of accessibility. Then what is the difference of those anaphoric forms? Take intermediate accessibility markers as an example. Pronoun and demonstrative NP both are intermediate accessibility markers. What is their difference? One cannot tell their difference based on AT.

Generally speaking, AT cannot interpret Chinese anaphora thoroughly, though it has revealed some characteristics of the anaphora.

Many researchers have recognized that point, and consequently try to seek other ways to improve the research when they apply AT to study Chinese anaphora. Y. Xu (2004) integrates the accessibility markers with the topicality of the antecedent to interpret Chinese anaphora. Jiang (2004) makes use of the degree of accessibility and syntactic positions to establish zero anaphor resolution. But their improvements still cannot interpret Chinese anaphora fully, because the previous research doesn't jump out of the AT framework. In other words, the previous research which applies AT to analyze Chinese anaphora cannot succeed in avoiding the limitations of AT. As a result, the research cannot interpret the uses of Chinese anaphoric forms exactly.

### 2.2.4 Anaphora Research Influenced by Cognitive Grammar Theory

#### 2.2.4.1 Overview

Cognitive Grammar (CG) also plays a role in Chinese anaphora research. Xiong (1998) and Weng (2006) both study Chinese anaphora with cognitive grammar approach. The latter is examined in detail as follows.

Weng (2006) studies zero anaphora in Chinese written narratives by applying van Hoek's reference point model.

She firstly proposes two criteria for the delimitation of dominion at the discourse level: 1) A dominion is ended when switch of reference occurs; or 2) A dominion is ended when the same referent which remains the reference point in both the preceding clause and the current clause is referred to by an NP, showing the low accessibility of the referent.

Secondly she investigates quantitative examples to analyze the occurrence and distribution of zero anaphora and the antecedent in Chinese. Based on that analysis, she suggests that two notions—the Prominence Hierarchy and the Macro-Connectivity—are crucial to account for zero anaphora resolution in Chinese narratives.

The Prominence Hierarchy denotes the prominence of the discourse referents in different positions, which is shown below: Subject- Subject > Object-Subject > Subject-Object > Modifier of the Subject-Subject > Topic-Subject / Object-Object > Nominal in the existential / presentative sentence-Subject.

The Macro-Connectivity refers to the intra-dominion or inter-dominion macro-connectivity. Intra-dominion macro-connectivity refers to the connectivity between the embedded clause and the projected clauses in the embedded dominion. And inter-dominion macro-connectivity refers to the connectivity among the clauses in different dominions. Weng also believes that the connectivity between dominions in discourse would not only influence the choice of anaphoric forms, but also help the reader resolve zero anaphora.

In terms of the Prominence Hierarchy and the Macro-Connectivity, Weng comes up with three Recovery Principles. And she further tests those three Recovery Principles with natural language data, and obtains a 99.87% correction rate on zero anaphora in Chinese.

#### 2.2.4.2 Evaluations

Using Cognitive Grammar to analyze Chinese anaphora is a kind of the cognitive approach to anaphora research. But since that theory much relies on the cognition, it is difficult for people to have a unified understanding on anaphora research. Hence it will not be used to interpret the uses of Chinese anaphoric forms in this thesis.

### 2.2.5 Anaphora Research with a CT Approach

#### 2.2.5.1 Overview

The proposal of CT that there is a correlation between the referring expression and the center of an utterance has attracted many researchers to use it and analyze Chinese anaphoric forms. This has been done from both the non-computational perspective as well as the computational perspective (Cf. Hu and Pan (2001, 2002), Cui (2004), Xu (2008), Xu et al. (2008), Yeh and Chen (2005), Cui et al. (2006), Wang (2006), Hu (2007)).

It is noted that CT is more widely applied in computational linguistics, in that it is a computational model of discourse interpretation. It only uses the surface information in sentences and does not need a huge amount of common sense knowledge to resolve pronouns. As a result it is relatively easy to implement on computational processes and has indeed been often used to analyze discourse anaphora in many languages.

Yeh and Chen (2005) resolve Chinese zero pronouns in a corpus which is part-of-speech tagged and shallow-parsed. They focus on zero pronouns occurring at the topic, subject, and object positions in utterances delimited by commas. They employ CT and its constraint rules to identify antecedents.

Cui et al. (2006) explores various factors involved in zero anaphora resolution in Chinese discourses based on CT. It distinguishes three types of utterances and uses clauses as the units of the resolution, which enables the authors to process inter-utterance and intra-utterance anaphora in a uniform way.

The paper further investigates the impact of the grammatical functions on the assignment of antecedents when two zero pronouns or more occur in the same utterance.

Wang (2006) and Hu (2007) are two Ph. D theses on Chinese anaphora resolution in CT framework, which will be examined in detail next. Besides that, Hu and Pan (2002) and Y. Xu (2008) are two representative works to apply CT from the non-computational perspective and also will be reviewed.

**1. Hu and Pan (2002)**

Hu and Pan (2002) argues that the CT framework needs to be further extended and revised for Chinese. The paper proposes to distinguish the backward-looking center ($C_b$) from the discourse segment topic (DST), and provides a more restrictive definition for $C_b$. Under their analysis, $C_b(U_i)$ is the element in $C_f(U_{i-1})$ that is realized by the matrix subject pronoun or the pronoun contained in the subject in $U_i$. They also argue that there is a division of labour between $C_b$ and DST. $C_b$ is used to track the focus of a sentence, whereas DST is used to track the focus of a discourse segment. When DST is identified in a discourse segment, it will not change within the same discourse segment. However, $C_b$ needs to be identified in every sentence, and it may change from sentence to sentence.

**2. Y. Xu (2008)**

CT takes a parametric approach, where the concepts and the notion can be adjusted according to the specific language. Implementation of CT and evaluation of the claims it makes in accounting for local coherence and pronominalization in discourse crucially hinge on the specification of the basic concepts and notions adopted in the theory, such as "utterance", "discourse segment", "realization", "salience" and "Rule 1 for pronoun". Xu (2008) introduces Poesio et al.'s (2004) parametric approach to CT, presents and compares the major results of its different instantiations, and suggests ways in which it can be further improved.

**3. Wang (2006)**

Wang (2006) studies anaphora resolution in Chinese with a centering approach. He only takes zero anaphora and the third-person pronominal anaphora as his object of inquiry.

In Wang (2006), he reformulates CT to study the zero pronoun in Chinese. Wang firstly extends the theoretical framework to include intra-sentential and long-distance anaphora, so as to improve the resolution algorithm.

Secondly, Wang applies CT to Chinese and instantiates the centering parameters within Chinese by generalizing a framework—Centering Model for Chinese (CMC). Wang uses CMC to analyze the anaphora in intra-sentential structure and global structure. For intra-sentential anaphora resolution, his strategy is to break a sentence into a structural sequence of sub-sentential units, each of which is the "utterance" in inter-sentential centering. For long-distance anaphora, his strategy is to compute the veins structures of the discourse segment and resolve the anaphora along its Domain of Referential Accessibility. Furthermore, Wang combines the strategies of intra-sentential anaphora and long-distance anaphora and obtains an extended version of anaphora resolution algorithm for Chinese.

Based on the extended version of anaphora resolution algorithm for Chinese, Wang carries out an empirical study. He chooses 30 texts from 5 genres – novel text, prose text, fairy tale text, news report text, and academic article text. And the success rate of his algorithm is 84.85%. Finally, Wang (2006) also analyzes the possible reasons of the unresolved anaphors.

**4. Hu (2007)**

Hu (2007) empirically explores the way that a zero pronoun refers to its antecedent, and implements systems which automatically resolve Chinese zero anaphora.

Hu (2007) firstly proposes that the clause can serve as the basic unit of analysis which can be defined on the basis of one predicate-argument structure. A zero pronoun occurs if an obligatory argument of a predicate is absent from the surface structure of a clause to which the predicate corresponds.

Hu (2007) further categorizes zero anaphora into intra- and inter-clausal anaphora, and explores the grammatical and pragmatic correlations held between a zero pronoun and its antecedent based on the notions of empty categories and binding principles [Chomsky (1981, 1982)], which are expressed in terms of the paths between a zero pronoun and its antecedent, and the categories of these paths.

Based on the above discussion, Hu (2007) implements two systems for zero anaphora resolution. One system operates within the framework of CT. By taking advantage of the hierarchical structure of a discourse, she extends the centering algorithm in such a way that Cp is the preferred interpretation of a zero pronoun in both inter- and intra-clausal anaphora. The other system makes use of a machine-learning algorithm, the decision tree, to resolve zero anaphora. It is revealed that while the factors representing the predictions based on CT capture the anaphora related to salience, those characterizing categories of the relation between a zero pronoun and its antecedent candidate capture the anaphora with other correlations. Several decision tree-based systems outperform the system based on CT.

Finally, Hu (2007) concludes that the resolution of zero anaphora is not only a matter of the competition of saliency, but also related to the grammatical and pragmatic correlations between a zero pronoun and its antecedent. The hierarchical structure of a discourse is a significant factor in the assessment of salience and correlations. Hu points out that the systems present promising results in the resolution of zero anaphora in Chinese discourse by taking the hierarchical structure of a discourse into account.

#### 2.2.5.2 Limitations of Centering Theory

CT contends that there is a correlation between the attentional status and referring expressions of nominals. But CT will encounter some problems when it is used to interpret Chinese anaphoric forms.

First, CT is not motivated by the anaphora, and therefore it is hard to interpret anaphora profoundly.

There is just a small part of CT which is related with the anaphora directly. CT only gives a prediction on the $C_b$ of being realized as a pronoun. As the anaphor is not necessarily the $C_b$, CT cannot interpret the uses of different anaphoric forms if the anaphoric forms are not $C_b$s.

Even though the anaphor is the $C_b$, CT still cannot capture the anaphora wholly. There are many different kinds of pronouns in Chinese: zero pronoun, the third-person pronoun, and so on. How to interpret different uses of those different pronouns? CT cannot give the answer.

Second, CT cannot cover all kinds of Chinese anaphora.

On one hand, CT only studies the phenomenon which occurs in a local segment. But there is some anaphora which will be beyond a local segment and belongs to the long distance anaphora ever mentioned in Wang (2006). CT cannot interpret such kind of Chinese anaphora.

The previous research on Chinese anaphora also expects to improve the application of CT. For instance, Wang (2006) extends CT from the local segment to the global segment, and Hu (2007) add some other factors such as rhetorical relations to CT. The previous research indeed improves the result of Chinese anaphora resolution. But the result leaves much to be desired. The success rate of zero pronoun resolution in Hu (2007) is only 82.96%. It can be found from the previous research that the application of CT has some limitations on the interpretations of different Chinese anaphoric forms.

### 2.2.6 Evaluations of Anaphora Research on Chinese

This section has examined some major research of discourse anaphora in Chinese. I have classified the relevant studies into five groups: neo-Gricean, functional, the AT, CG, and CT approaches. In the neo-Gricean approach, Pu (1998) makes use of neo-Gricean framework to analyze Chinese anaphora. In the functional approach, J. Xu applies Rhetorical Structure Theory (RST) to study zero, pronoun, and noun phrase anaphora in Chinese. Taking an AT approach, Xu and Jiang explore various features of anaphora in Chinese based on AT, and Ding (2005) studies some accessibility markers in Chinese according to the idea of AT. Weng (2006) concentrates on zero anaphora in Chinese within Cognitive Grammar framework with CG approach. And Hu and Pan (2002), Yeh and Chen (2005), Cui et al. (2006), Wang (2006), Hu (2007), Xu (2008) all investigate Chinese anaphora with the CT approach.

It can be seen that most of the previous studies on Chinese anaphora are influenced by English anaphora research, and the impact is especially strong for these three theories: AT (Accessibility Theory), CT (Centering Theory), and RST (Rhetorical Structure Theory).

Though previous research on Chinese anaphora has made many strides in interpreting Chinese anaphoric forms, the issue is far from being well understood. I believe that two areas may account for the insufficient interpretations of Chinese anaphoric forms: a) which factors that can affect the uses of Chinese anaphoric forms have not been thoroughly identified in the previous research, and b) how these factors play a role in the uses of anaphoric forms has not been properly understood in the previous research.

## 2.3 Summary

This chapter makes an overview of anaphora research on English as well as on Chinese. English anaphora research from the discourse perspective is reviewed in terms of functional, cognitive, semantic, and computational approaches, while Chinese anaphora research from the discourse perspective is reviewed in terms of the neo-Gricean, functional, AT, CG, and CT approaches. Advantages as well as drawbacks with each of the major approaches are analyzed, as are the major studies applying these theories. Overall, we can see that although there is a lot of progress made by earlier researchers, there is a still a lot of factors in Chinese anaphora that need further exploration.

# Chapter 3 Interpreting Chinese Anaphoric Forms

This chapter addresses the issue of how to interpret distinctive uses of various Chinese anaphoric forms with the framework of information accessibility. A crucial step is to figure out what factors there are and how they affect uses of Chinese anaphoric forms. Hence the first section discusses the factors that have been identified as affecting uses of Chinese anaphoric forms in previous research. The second part proposes a new set of factors affecting uses of Chinese anaphoric forms. The third section illustrates how the main factors proposed by this thesis affect uses of Chinese anaphoric forms. And the last section gives a summary.

## 3.1 Common Features of the Factors Suggested by the Past Work

Researchers have suggested numerous factors and theories to account for the interpretations of Chinese anaphoric forms.① Huang (1994) argues that pragmatic factors are fundamental for the interpretations of Chinese anaphoric forms. Chen (1986, 1987) believes that discourse structure is a key factor to affect the uses of zero pronouns. Pu (1998) argues the following factors determining the occurrence and distribution of zero anaphors in Chinese: cognitive constraints, discourse context, pragmatic and semantic information, and speaker/writer-audience interaction. J. Xu (2002, 2003) suggests different factors for different anaphoric

① The detail introduction has been mentioned in chapter 2.

forms, in which the main factors include referential distance, lexical meaning, discourse structure established through rhetorical relations, and pragmatic factors. Shen (2002), Y. Xu (2004), Jiang (2004), Ding (2005), and Weng (2006) all interpret Chinese anaphoric forms in terms of accessibility and some other factors. And Wang (2006) and Hu (2007) mainly use the topic and in the CT framework to analyze the uses of Chinese anaphoric forms especially the zero pronoun.

Among various factors proposed in the previous research, the term "accessibility" is a general term which includes four sub-factors: distance, topic, saliency, and discourse structure①. And "cognitive constraints" in Pu (1998) are actually some kind of the representation of "accessibility". Hence altogether there are five kinds of proposed factors in the previous research: distance, topic, saliency, discourse structure, and pragmatic roles, which are shown below.

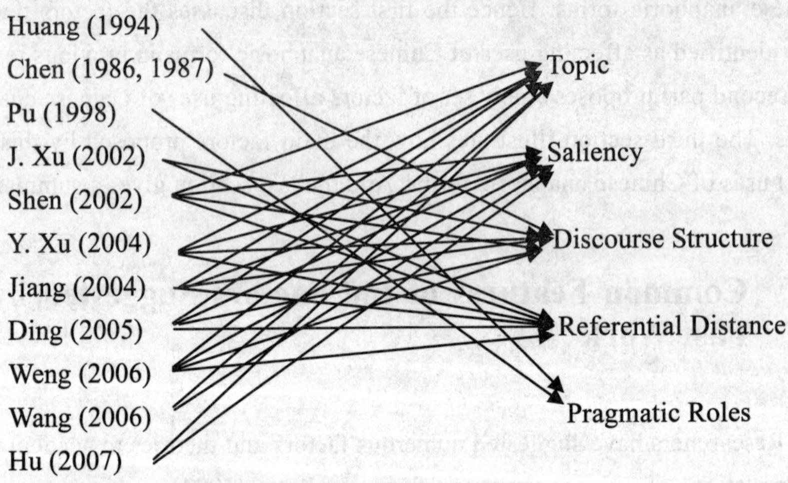


**Fig. 3.1　Various Factors Suggested in the Previous Research**

It can be viewed from Fig. 3.1 that there is a complicated representation about proposed factors in the previous research. The factors—topic, saliency, discourse structure, and referential distance—have been suggested by most of the previous research, while the factor "pragmatic roles" has received relatively less mention in the previous research. I think the different views on the factors are rooted in the basic views of different researchers on language mechanism.

① Ariel (1990) terms the factor discourse structure as 'unity'.

It is believed that every kind of expressions has its own distinct semantic meaning and consequently has its distinguished structural behaviors in theoretical linguistics, which is fundamental and cannot be violated in pragmatic level. But in pragmatic linguistics, it is believed that different kinds of expressions are resulted from different purposes in the communication. I contend the view of the theoretical linguistics. Therefore different Chinese anaphoric forms are regarded as the requirement of the language mechanism rather than the result of the pragmatic uses in this thesis. And pragmatic factors will not be taken into account in this thesis, though they can affect the uses of Chinese anaphoric forms to a certain degree for some personal intentions.

Other proposed factors, topic, discourse structure, salience, and referential distance, are all related to uses of Chinese anaphoric forms from language uses, and thus will be considered by this thesis. It seems that those proposed factors vary and their effects on uses of Chinese anaphoric forms differ. In fact they can be regarded to have a common feature; that is the *accessibility*, the nuclear concept of Accessibility Theory. In other words, the concept accessibility can unify all kinds of proposed factors and provide a general account for uses of Chinese anaphoric forms.

In a word, accessibility is the essential point for the interpretation of various Chinese anaphoric forms. And this thesis will thus interpret Chinese anaphoric forms based on accessibility.

## 3.2 Factors Affecting the Use of Chinese Anaphoric Forms

This section focuses on the factors that can affect the uses of Chinese anaphoric forms.

### 3.2.1 The Accessibility for the Interpretations of Anaphoric Forms

It is usually suggested that different anaphoric forms have different distributions. Loosely speaking, pronouns are used most often when the referent is represented in a prominent way in the minds of the discourse participants, but more fully specified forms are needed when the representation of the referent is less prominent. Various terms have been used to describe that phenomenon: "salience", "accessibility", "topicality", "focus of attention",[①] or "activation". The terms are not strictly synonymous, but they are similar in that they attribute choices in reference forms to the cognitive status of the referents.

The general cognitive status of a referent is actually the "accessibility" proposed in Accessibility Theory. Many behaviors of a referent can result in different cognitive status and affect the accessibility of itself in people's cognitive psychology.

I believe that the accessibility can generally reveal the semantic variability and explain different distributions of various Chinese anaphoric forms, in that anaphora is a kind of discourse phenomenon involving the cognition after all. When an entity, which is prominent in cognitive status, is referred back, it can be detected more easily and the anaphoric link can be established more easily. And when an entity which is not prominent is referred back, it will not be detected so easily and the anaphoric link will be established relatively difficultly. The term "accessibility" can exactly represent the impact of cognitive status of entities on anaphora understanding which will put further constraint on the uses of anaphoric forms.

So this thesis will interpret Chinese anaphoric forms based on the accessibility, in which what factors will affect the accessibility of the antecedent is the prominent question of the interpretations of different Chinese anaphoric forms. More concretely speaking, the factors which can affect the accessibility of the antecedent will finally require different Chinese anaphoric forms to encode different degrees of accessibility.

In addition, there are two other concepts which are often mentioned in the

① "Focus of attention" is not the same as the term "focus" which is used in descriptions of information structure, and roughly refers to the new, highlighted information in a sentence. Instead, "focus of attention" refers to the item which is currently most salient in the discourse in terms of pronoun reference, which corresponds more to the discourse topic than the focus.

previous anaphora research and are often confused with the accessibility. One concept is the inference load, and the other is discourse coherence. This thesis will describe the difference and the correlation between those two concepts and the accessibility.

The inference load and the accessibility, in my view, are two sides of one thing. Given the degree of accessibility of an antecedent is low in people's cognition, people are hard to make the anaphor access the antecedent, and thus the inference load from the anaphor to the antecedent is naturally heavy, and vise versa. So there is an inverse relation between inference load and accessibility degree: the heavier is the inference load from the anaphor to the antecedent, the lower is the degree of accessibility of the antecedent; while the lighter is the inference load, the higher is the degree of accessibility. Some previous research ever analyzes the anaphora according to the inference load from the antecedent to the anaphor. Centering Theory, for instance, proposes that there are different inference loads in different Center Transition and those inference loads further affect uses of referring expressions. Actually the approach of inference load and that of the accessibility get the same conclusion from different perspectives.

Discourse coherence is the other concept which is often proposed to interpret anaphoric forms in the previous research. Some research believes that discourse coherence is related to uses of various anaphoric forms. But the concept 'discourse coherence' is actually a vague concept. There is no clear definition of discourse coherence. Most researchers view discourse coherence as a semantic concept. And they usually suggest that the text with light inference load and high degree of accessibility is more coherent than the text with heavy inference load and low degree of accessibility. So it can be clearly seen that discourse coherence is often correlated with inference load and the accessibility in the previous research.

To sum up, accessibility, the inference load, and discourse coherence interact with each other, which can explain why they all are mentioned in the previous research on anaphora. But this thesis will only analyze Chinese anaphoric forms from the point of accessibility, because the accessibility is the fundamental cause of different uses of Chinese anaphoric forms.

### 3.2.2 What Factors Can Affect the Accessibility of the Antecedent

There has been very little discussion on the factors which can affect the accessibility of the antecedent in the previous research.

It seems that the factors which can affect the accessibility of the antecedent can be revealed more clearly through the process of anaphora understanding. Anaphora includes two ingredients (the antecedent and the anaphor) and one anaphoric relation between two ingredients. The anaphora understanding is actually a course of the access from the anaphor to the antecedent. Only when the anaphora is understood, the anaphor can access to the antecedent; otherwise the anaphor cannot access the antecedent. So any factor affecting anaphora understanding will affect the access from the anaphor to the antecedent and moreover affect the accessibility of the antecedent.

It is usually believed that both antecedent and anaphor should be included in anaphora understanding. But I argue that not only the antecedent and the anaphor but also two clauses in which the antecedent and the anaphor occur respectively should be taken into account in anaphora understanding, which is illustrated below.

(3.1) a. Yi ge duiyuan$_i$ daoguajingou jiang qiu da ru wang nei,

b. ta$_i$ xihuan guangjie.

"A player hits the ball into the net with a bicycle kick. He likes shopping."

In the above example (3.1), the NP *yi ge duiyuan* in (3.1a) and the pronoun *ta* in (3.1b) could have the same referent. But it is still difficult to understand the anaphoric relation between them. Why? The main problem is that it is hard to understand the whole text in example (3.1). The clause (3.1a) expresses a kind of information which is greatly different from that expressed by (3.1b). Hence it is hard for readers to accommodate (3.1a & b) into a discourse and establish an anaphoric link between two NPs occurring in (3.1a) and (3.1b) respectively.

It can be seen from example (3.1) that not only the antecedent and the anaphor but also the relation between two clauses where the antecedent and the anaphor occur respectively can affect the anaphora understanding. Hence, the variations of anaphora on the antecedent, the anaphor, and the clauses included by anaphora all should be taken into account in the factors which can affect the accessibility of the antecedent.

Thus, the accessibility of the antecedent can be affected by three aspects: the antecedent, the anaphor, and the relation between the clauses where the antecedent and the anaphor occur.

#### 3.2.2.1 The Impact of Discourse Structure on the Accessibility of the Antecedent

This thesis argues that the relation between the clauses in which the antecedent and the anaphor occur respectively can affect the accessibility of the antecedent from the hierarchical perspective. This thesis terms the factor which is related to the hierarchical relation between two clauses of anaphora as discourse structure.

Different discourse structures between two clauses where the antecedent and the anaphor occur respectively will have different impacts on the accessibility of the antecedent, in that they can result in different loads of accommodating those two clauses into a whole and affect the specific access from the anaphor to the antecedent. For instance,

(3.2) a. Laozhang$_i$ zhuyuan le,

b. Yinwei zuotian Ø$_i$ shuai le yi jiao.

"Laozhang is at hospital, for he had a tumbling yesterday."

(3.3) a. Yinwei zuotian xia xue,

b. lu shang tai hua,

c. Laozhang$_i$ shuai le yi jiao,

d. *ta* $_i$ houlai zhuyuan le.

"It snowed yesterday. The road was so slippery that Laozhang slipped down and had to go to hospital."

The meanings which are represented by (3.2a & b) or (3.3c & d) are almost the same. But their relations are different due to different texts. In the respect of semantic relations, (3.2b) is the cause of (3.2a), while (3.3a) to (3.3b) is the causc of (3.3c) and moreover (3.3c) is the cause of (3.3d).

Thus, it can be seen from the above two examples that two clauses which represent a similar meaning have different discourse structures in different contexts. Different discourse structures make the accommodations of two clauses which represent the similar meaning different. (3.2a & b) are easily accommodated by a strong logical relation *yinwei*, while (3.3c & d) are relative difficultly accommodated. As a consequence, the access from the anaphor to the antecedent also differs in those two clauses, and the degree of accessibility of the antecedent *laozhang* in (3.2a) is different from the antecedent in (3.3c).

In general, discourse structure is closely related to the accessibility of the antecedent. It can determine the relation between two clauses of anaphora and further impact the accessibility of the antecedent. And it is consequently one of the main factors which will affect uses of different Chinese anaphoric forms.

#### 3.2.2.2 The Impact of the Topicality on the Accessibility of the Antecedent

It has been suggested in the above text that the antecedent and the anaphor both can affect the accessibility of the antecedent. How do they affect the accessibility? At first blush it seems that there are many possibilities. But in fact there are only two kinds of influence: one is the antecedent and the anaphor affect the accessibility of the antecedent from the discourse perspective; and the other is they affect the accessibility of the antecedent from the clause perspective. It is because the antecedent and the anaphor always occur in some clauses as well as in a discourse. This part discusses the impact of the antecedent and the anaphor on the accessibility of the antecedent from the discourse perspective.

Both the antecedent and the anaphor discussed in this paper are nominal expressions, as mentioned in chapter 1. Since all nominal expressions in a discourse constitute information flow of the discourse, different nominal expressions will have distinct impacts on people's cognition due to their respective information.

Every nominal expression has its own descriptive information which is encoded by its lexical expression. But besides the descriptive information, every nominal expression will have other kind of information which is resulted from its features in information flow. It has been suggested in Halliday (1975) that the information of nominal expressions of a discourse can be analyzed from people's cognition. For instance, the information which is mentioned many times differs with the information which is mentioned for the first time from people's cognition, for the occurring times of the former information can promote its cognitive status.

The information resulted from people's cognition is important for discourse understanding. The previous research has categorized the information into various sub-types from different viewpoints: topic vs. non-topic, focus of attentional state vs. non-focus of attentional state, given vs. new, salient vs. non-salient, activated vs. brand, focus vs. background, etc.

The given-new distinction and the activated-non-activated distinction are actually proposed from the same perspective. Those two kinds of information are differentiated according to whether an expression has occurred in the preceding discourse. Given a discourse referent is introduced into a discourse for the first time; it is usually viewed as a new or non-activated referent. Given a discourse referent has been introduced into a discourse more than one time, it is given/activated. Some research argues that there is semi-given/semi-activated information between the given/activated and the new/non-activated information, for some expressions can be bridged through the inference to some other expressions which have occurred in the discourse. For example, the expression *men* (door) can be inferred from the expression *fangzi* (house) for there is usually a door in a house, and consequently the former expression is semi-given/semi-activated even if it is introduced at the first time, given *fangzi* (house) has occurred in the discourse.

The focus-backgrounds and focus-non-focus distinction both pay attention to whether an expression is the focus of the attentional state. The topic vs. non-topic distinction is differentiated according to whether an expression is a topic. The salient vs. non-salient distinction is differentiated according to whether an expression is salient or not in people's cognition.

Nominal expressions of a discourse always have some kind of the above information from people's cognition, which can be illustrated below.

(3.4) Zhuozi shang you *yi ben shu*. *Na* shi yi ben youguan yuyanxue de shu.

"There is a book on the table which is a linguistic book."

In example (3.4), two expressions *yi ben shu* (this book) and *na* (that) have different information in respect of whether the information is given or new. The discourse referent expressed by *yi ben shu* (this book) occurs in the discourse for the first time, and therefore *yi ben shu* (this book) belongs to the new information. The discourse referent expressed by *na* (that) is the same with that expressed by *yi ben shu* (this book), so the information expressed by *na* (that) belongs to the given information.

A referent can express different kinds of information. For instance, the expression which is a topic is usually the given information, because the information in the common background of a discourse more easily becomes the topic. And the expression which is a topic is also usually the focus of the attentional state, because the topic is expected to be continued, and the topic is thus the focus of the attention state of the writer. It can be indicated that there are some common features in different kinds of information.

Many kinds of information among the above information have been used to analyze the use of anaphoric forms. Gundel et al. (1993) makes use of given information of antecedents to analyze uses of different anaphoric forms in English. Centering Theory (CT) proposes that the focus[①] of attentional state, which actually includes two kinds of information: the topicality and the saliency, can affect the choice of referring expression.[②] Ariel (1990), J. Xu (2002), Y. Xu (2002), etc. all suggest the topic to interpret the uses of anaphoric forms.

In my opinion, the topic vs. non-topic distinction, or to say the topicality of the antecedent and the anaphor, will play the most important role in the interpretations of Chinese anaphoric forms.

With regard to the given-new distinction, there is no clear correspondence between expressions and the given-new information. Hence it is difficult to establish a reliable Givenness Hierarchy on different Chinese nominal expressions.

As for the focus/non-focus information, it mixes two factors—the topicality and the saliency. And consequently it is inappropriate for the interpretations of Chinese anaphoric forms, too.

---

① To be noted that the term *focus* has been used to represent different aspects in various linguistic fields. The *focus* here refers to the focus of attentional state.

② In Centering Theory, the topicality is termed "topic" and the saliency is termed "salience".

As far as topical/non-topical information is concerned, it can be used to analyze anaphoric forms. Anaphora is a device to make discourse referents continuous in information flow of a discourse. Information flow is primarily concerned with what a discourse is about. Namely, information flow mainly reflects the topics of a discourse, either topic coherence or topic shift. As the antecedent and the anaphor both are components of information flow, whether they are topics or not will result in different status in people's cognition. As a result, the topicality of the antecedent and the anaphor will affect the accessibility of the antecedent.

In short, the factor topicality can affect the accessibility of the antecedent and then plays an important role in the interpretations of Chinese anaphoric forms. Hence the behaviors of the antecedent and the anaphor on the topicality will be seriously considered in this thesis.

#### 3.2.2.3 The Impact of the Saliency on the Accessibility of the Antecedent

It has been suggested that the antecedent and the anaphor will affect the uses of Chinese anaphoric forms either from the discourse perspective or from the clause perspective. From the discourse perspective, whether the antecedent and the anaphor are the topicality can affect the accessibility of the antecedent, which is posed in last part. This part will discuss the impact of the antecedent and the anaphor on the interpretations of Chinese anaphoric forms from the clause perspective.

Generally speaking, the expression which takes the subject position of a clause will be more prominent than the expression which takes the object position according to the capture of a clause. The cognitive status of an expression from the clausal perspective is termed **the saliency**. Hence the expression in the subject position is more salient than the expression in the object position in people's cognition. In general, different entities which take different positions of a clause vary in the saliency. Logically speaking, the more salient is an entity, the easier it is for people to capture.

As far as the anaphora is concerned, the variations of the antecedent and the anaphor in positions will result in different saliency which can affect the capture of the antecedent and the anaphor in people's cognition. If an antecedent and its anaphor both are more salient, both of them will be more easily captured, and the anaphor can access the antecedent more easily; otherwise the anaphor will access the antecedent more difficultly. Thus, the saliency can affect the accessibility of the antecedent.

In short, the saliency of the antecedent and the anaphor can affect the access from the anaphor to the antecedent. And hence it is also an important factor which can affect the accessibility of the antecedent.

#### 3.2.2.4 The Impact of Referential Distance on the Accessibility of the Antecedent

Linearity is commonly known to impact the uses of anaphoric forms. Li (1985), for instance, finds that the percentage of zero anaphors drops sharply with the number of intervening clauses increasing.

It can be said that the impact of linearity on the uses of anaphoric forms is rooted in the impact of recency in people's cognition, which can affect the access from the anaphor to the antecedent. Generally speaking, the more recent is the antecedent, the easier it is for people to access the antecedent from the anaphor.

This thesis terms the recency as referential distance. Thus, referential distance between the antecedent and the anaphor can also affect the accessibility of the antecedent through the impact on the access from the anaphor to the antecedent. The more distant the antecedent is for the anaphor, the less recent it is, hence the less accessible it is.

### 3.2.3 Factors in Interpretations of Chinese Anaphoric Forms

Four factors are argued to affect the accessibility of the antecedent: discourse structure, the topicality, the saliency, and referential distance, and are consequently important for the interpretations of Chinese anaphoric forms.

In fact, those four factors describe different impacts of different aspects of anaphora on the accessibility of the antecedent. Discourse structure pays attention to the impact of the hierarchical relations between two clauses in anaphora on the accessibility of the antecedent. The topicality is concerned with the impact of the cognitive status of the antecedent or the anaphor being the topic in discourse information flow. The saliency concerns the impact of cognitive status of the antecedent or the anaphor from the clausal perspective. And referential distance gives attention to the impact of the linear distance between the antecedent and the anaphor.

To sum up, discourse structure, the topicality, the saliency, and referential distance can affect the accessibility of the antecedent from many aspects of anaphora, and hence should be four main factors of interpretations of Chinese anaphoric forms.

## 3.3 Discourse Structure and the Accessibility of the Antecedent

It is evident that the factor discourse structure will affect the accessibility of the antecedent, and further affect the uses of Chinese anaphoric forms. This section will explore how discourse structure affects the accessibility of the antecedent and the uses of Chinese anaphoric forms.

### 3.3.1 Past Work on Discourse Structure

How to establish discourse structure of two clauses in anaphora is the first step for the impact of discourse structure on the accessibility of the antecedent. So this part chiefly reviews some prominent research on discourse structure.

There is much research on discourse structure which can be roughly classified into two categories: one is the research from the semantic approach; and the other is the research from the generative approach.

The semantic approach to discourse structure chiefly proposes that there is some semantic relation between two elementary constituents of a discourse. Rhetorical Structure Theory (RST) is the representative theory which analyzes discourse structure from the semantic approach.[①] The main claim of RST is that the textual organization and the coherence are characterized in terms of rhetorical relations that hold between different units of a text (so-called text spans).

① Chapter 2 has reviewed RST in detail.

Rhetorical relations are actually various semantic relations such as Background, Circumstance, and so on, which has been described in detail in chapter 2 of this thesis.

The generative approach to discourse structure follows the generative view and proposes that a discourse is generated by some elementary units through several rules. Livia (1996) is the representative work. We shall take a close look at the generative approach to discourse structure in Livia (1996).

Livia (1996) proposes a Linguistic Mode of Discourse (LMD) based on the assumption that a discourse can be built with the structural/generative methodology. Livia brings forward that there are two new elementary linguistic units: the propositional discourse constituent unit (dcu) and the non-propositional discourse operator. Dcu is a contextually indexed representation of information. Each dcu expresses an event or in general a state of affairs in some spatio-temporal location, involving some set of (defined or as of yet undefined) participants. For example the sentence *I went downtown but Mary stayed home* is analyzed as a three unit structure consisting of two dcus *(I went downtown* and *Mary stayed home)* and a discourse operator *but,* a logical connective which asserts the relationship between two states of affairs.

Based on dcus and discourse operators, a discourse can be analyzed with the discourse parse tree (DPT) which takes propositional dcus at the leaves. Moreover, three basic types of higher structures will be distinguished: Coordination, Subordination, and Binary constructions. Nonterminal nodes of the DPT will always be one of these, and will be labeled by *C, S,* or *B* accordingly.

Coordination refers to the process of continuing the development. And Subordination includes the structural manners in which discourse activities interrupt the completion of other ongoing activities. Therefore some rhetorical relations such as Elaborations, Digressions, Asides, and Appositives will be viewed as subordination in Livia's research. Binary structures is constructed according to binary relations which hold between two constituents related logically (e.g. if/then, then/if, or, therefore), rhetorically, (e.g. sum up), or interactionally (e.g. question/answer, warrant/response, error/repair). Those three kinds of higher structures can be illustrated below.

(3.5) I like to read Sci-Fi. I like to ski and I like to sleep late.

(3.6) I like to do fun things on vacation. I like to read Sci-Fi. I like to ski and I like to sleep late.

(3.7) The airport has been closed, for there is a heavy snow.

The structures of (3.5-3.7) can be characterized by the tree given in (3.8-3.10).

(3.8)

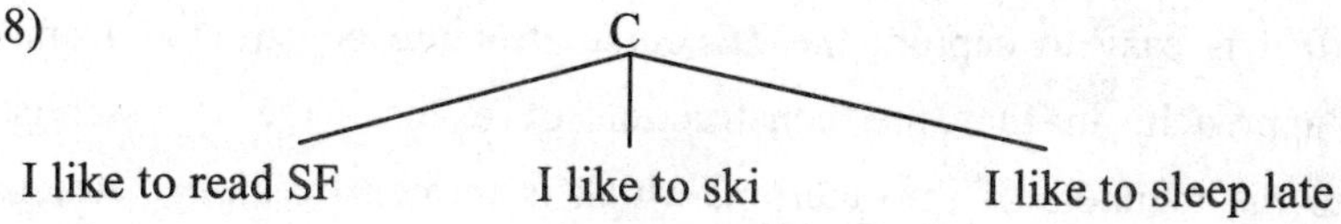


(3.9)

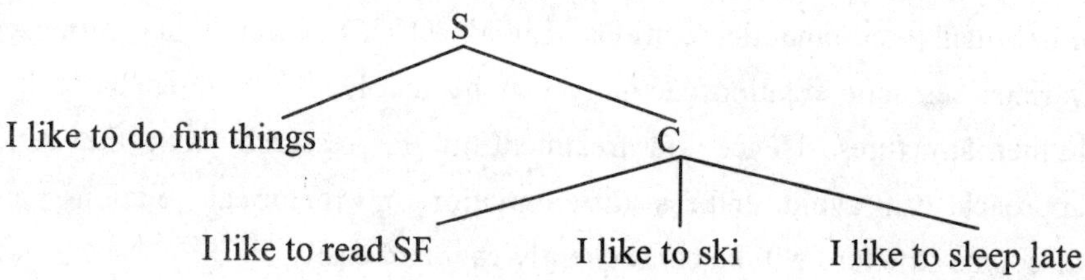


(3.10)

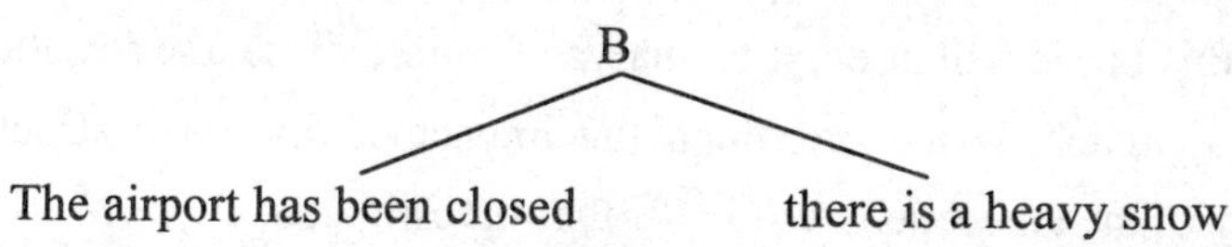


Based on dcus and three kinds of higher structures, the linguistic structure of a discourse can be obtained.

There is always a dispute on the research from the semantic approach or from the generative approach. This thesis will not pay more attention on such dispute, but rather consider which approach to discourse structure can more benefit the interpretations of Chinese anaphoric forms.

The semantic approach to discourse structure is not suitable for the interpretations of Chinese anaphoric forms due to these two major problems: a) semantic connections between units are not easily distinguished and then are not easily controlled, and b) it is hard to determine how many rhetorical relations are needed in the interpretations of Chinese anaphoric forms; which has been discussed in chapter 2 of this thesis. Hence the semantic approach to discourse structure is not adequate for the interpretations of Chinese anaphoric forms.

The generative approach to discourse structure is a new attempt for the interpretations of Chinese anaphoric forms. There are two main advantages.

First, the discourse structure constructed from the generative approach is brief and clear, in that the construction rules are finite. There are only three kinds of higher structures which can connect various elementary units in Livia's (1996) research; whereas there are a lot of rhetorical relations in the research from the semantic approach. Therefore the discourse structure can be idealized greatly in the generative framework.

Second, it is easy to capture the discourse structure constructed from the generative approach, in that the construction of a discourse is established according to the manners of information, which is termed by higher structure, other than the semantic relations. Livia's (1996) research has proposed that various semantic relations actually can be involved into three basic kinds of higher structures. Hence the treatment in the research from the generative approach can avoid endless differentiation on rhetorical relations, and the discourse structure will be consequently captured easily.

Thus, this thesis will attempt to analyze Chinese discourse structure from the generative approach, based on which the impact of discourse structure on the accessibility of the antecedent will be further investigated.

### 3.3.2 The Construction of Chinese Discourse Structure

According to the generative view, a discourse is composed of elementary units with certain rules. Hence there are two important facets in the construction of discourse structure in Chinese: a) what are elementary units of Chinese discourses; and b) what are construction rules of discourse structure in Chinese. This sub-section will chiefly discuss the above two facets.

#### 3.3.2.1 The Basic Unit of a Discourse: the Clause

The basic unit of a discourse is the foundation of the analysis of discourse structure. In the previous research there are usually three main different views on the basic unit of a discourse: the *sentence*, the *clause*, and the *utterance*.

The basic unit of a discourse is suggested as the *sentence* in most of the previous research on discourse analysis in traditional Chinese linguistics, which is so-called the sentence-based analysis. A sentence is usually defined as a sequence of words constituting a statement, question, or a command that ends with a full stop when written down in Chinese. For example,

(3.11) a. Buguo, zhuanghuren zhi zhuanghuren you de shi fa.

b. Jiu jiang cuntou de lukou quan pai ren feng qilai sou shen, fan kuangkuangloulou.

"But, there are many methods to govern the farmers. Some farmers are demanded to guard all the roads of the village. Every farmer and his baskets will be searched every time he passes the roads."

In example (3.11), the text can be parsed into two basic units according to the sentence-based analysis, for there are two full stops.

But there is a major problem to regard the sentence as the basic unit of a Chinese discourse. In Chinese discourses, a sentence can include many actions or states. For instance, there are four actions in example (3.11b): *pai*, *feng*, *sou*, and *fan*. To take the sentence as the basic unit of a Chinese discourse will ignore the actions included in the sentence. So many researchers disagree with the sentence-based analysis and suggest the clause as the basic unit of a Chinese discourse. Such analysis is so-called the clause-based analysis.

J. Xu (2002) proposes a term *discourse clause* (篇章小句) to represent the basic unit of a Chinese discourse. The *discourse clause* is decided mainly by the structure of the subject and the predication. J. Xu also takes pause and function into account when judging *discourse clause*.

The clause-based analysis can catch the concrete events or states in a discourse, so it can reveal the detail processing of the discourse clearly. As a result, the clause-based analysis is adopted by many researchers. But the clause has not been clearly defined in the previous research yet.

The utterance is another concept which has ever been suggested as the basic unit of a discourse. Centering Theory suggests the *utterance* as the basic unit of a discourse. But there is no explicit definition on the *utterance* in CT. GJW95 takes a sentence with a full stop as an utterance, while Pan and Hu (2002) takes a clause as an utterance when applying CT to analyze Chinese discourses. It can be viewed that thc term utterance is actually not a new concept in Chinese discourse research. The utterance is generally regarded as the sentence or the clause.

There is another view on the basic unit of a discourse, which has not been mentioned in the previous research on Chinese discourses. Livia's Linguistic Discourse Model (LDM) uses a term *discourse constituent unit* (dcu) to represent the basic unit of a discourse. Moreover, LDM argues that dcu expresses a single event or state of affairs in some discourse world.

In my opinion, the basic unit of a discourse is actually the smallest component in discourse understanding. Generally speaking, a discourse is viewed as an integration which is made up of many actions or states and the participants. Hence the actions or the states are the key points of discourse understanding. And they should thus be analyzed as the basic unit of a discourse. Livia's definition of the basic unit of a discourse is just accordant with the above idea. Then this thesis will follow Livia's definition on the basic unit of a discourse. But this thesis would prefer to use the term *clause* to represent the basic unit of a discourse, for that can avoid the complexity of terms.

In all, this thesis argues that the basic unit of a discourse is a clause, which expresses a single event or state of affairs in some discourse world. For example,

(3.12)①Dajin wang zhe niang，/②jue de/③zhe tiao nan cai de miyu haishi bu hao cai //，④jiu lengzheng zhe wang zhe niang /。

"Dajin looked at Niang, and felt that that difficult riddle was still difficult to solve, and consequently was stunned and still looked at Niang."

(3.13)①Denglaotaiye 70 yu sui，/②bu shi zi/ er③xiaogubojin，/④bu zuo guan / er⑤shi guanchang zhi dao，/⑥bu shi yiren / er⑦ hui bian banshu cihua。

"Deng Lao Taiye was more than seventy years old. He could not read any word but he was knowledgeable. He was not an official but he knew the official rules. He was not an artist but he could tell some special stories."

In example (3.12), the discourse can be analyzed into four clauses which is split by slash "/" and marked by the number. The clause ③ is in the inside of the clause ② from the surface expression. But it is regarded as a clause, for '*zhe tiao nan cai de miyu haishi bu hao cai*' (this difficult riddle was still difficult to solve) expresses a single state of affairs. Example (3.13) has seven clauses correspondingly.

As to some special sentence patterns in Chinese, they also can be analyzed into clauses according to the above definition of the *clause*, which can be illustrated by some examples.

(3.14) Zhangsan chifan / shangke qu le.

"Zhangsan had lunch and went to school."

(3.15) Ta yunxu wo / ban zhe jian shi.

"She allowed me to carry that thing."

(3.16) Wei le wancheng lunwen, / ta riyijiye de xie.

"In order to complete the thesis, he worked day and night."

(3.14) is an example of Serial Verb Constructions. It would be analyzed as many clauses in a Serial Verb Construction, for each verb in the Serial Verb Construction represents a state of affairs.

(3.15) is an example of the Pivotal Construction. In the Pivotal Construction, there are two different verbs which will denote different states of affairs, and they will thus be analyzed into different clauses.

(3.16) is an example of the Complex Sentence which has a subordinate clause and a main clause. The Complex Sentence is regarded as an analysis unit in some literatures, and the anaphora in the Complex Sentence is usually viewed as the intra-sentential anaphora. But according to the definition of the clause in this thesis, the Complex Sentence can also be analyzed into many clauses according to the state of affairs. In example (3.16), the discourse is analyzed into two clauses: "*wancheng lunwen*" (to complete the thesis) and "*ta riyijiye de xie*" (he worked day and night), for "*wancheng lunwen*" (to complete the thesis) and "*ta riyijiye de xie*" (he worked day and night) express two different states of affairs.

In all, the basic unit of a Chinese discourse is argued as the clause in this thesis. A clause expresses either an event or a state.

#### 3.3.2.2 Higher Structures in Discourse Structure

Various clauses in a discourse will be combined according to some construction rules in the generative framework. Livia (1996) proposes that there are three basic types of higher structures with which various basic units are composed into complex units. Those three types of higher structures are Coordination, Subordination, and Binary.

Livia (1996) distinguishes three types of higher structures from structural relations rather than semantic relations between different discourse information: Coordination, Subordination, and Binary. But different semantic relations can be involved into a kind of higher structures. Coordination is analyzed as continuing the development of an ongoing discourse activity, which includes adding a next item to a list, giving a next episode of a story, beginning a new topic in a conversation when the discussion of a previous topic has been concluded, or going on to a next expected activity in a speech event. Subordination is analyzed as interrupting an ongoing activity, which includes five kinds of semantic relations: Elaborations, Digressions, Asides, Appositives, and Interruptions. Binary is analyzed as the structure with an explicit or implicit relation, which includes the following semantic relations: the logical, rhetorical, or interactional relations.

But I think that the description of the higher structures in Livia (1996) is not clear enough. This thesis will try to differentiate different higher structures more clearly. In my opinion, different information computations are actually distinct ways of discourse information processing.

As far as discourse information processing is concerned, the ways to process discourse information are limited. Given some discourse information, there are only three kinds of ways in which the discourse is developed: one is to continue the discourse information, the second is to interrupt the discourse information, and the third is to combine the discourse information with some new information through some logical relations. Those three kinds of higher structures, Coordination, Subordination, and Binary, are actually the structural representation of different ways of discourse information processing, in which each kind of higher structures is corresponding to one way of discourse information processing.

It is worth noting that the terms coordination and subordination have often been mentioned in the literatures with different meanings from that of this thesis. Specifically, both coordination and subordination are discussed from the perspective of semantic relations. For instance, some researchers differentiate complex sentences from simple sentences in Chinese. There are more than two clauses in a complex sentence. If a clause of a complex sentence depends on the other clause of the complex sentence semantically, the dependant clause is regarded as the subordinate clause and the other clause which is depended by the dependent clause is regarded as the main clause. Below is an example for a complex sentence.

(3.17) a. Dang tianqi yue lai yue nuanhe,

b. Tian jiu hei de yue lai yue wan.

"The warmer it is, the later the day gets dark."

The example (3.17) is a complex sentence. From the semantic meaning, (3.17a) is just a restrictor of (3.17b) and (3.17b) holds the crucial meaning of the complex sentence. Hence (3.17a) depends on (3.17b) semantically. (3.17a) is the subordinate clause of the complex sentence, whereas (3.17b) is the main clause of the complex sentence.

It should be obvious from example (3.17) that the subordination is commonly used from the semantic perspective in literatures. The coordination is the same with the subordination.

However, in this thesis the notions of coordination and subordination are given new meanings. Both coordination and subordination will be analyzed based on discourse information processing. They are used to reveal different ways of discourse information processing, and are consequently structural relations of different discourse information in this thesis. The term binary has not been mentioned in the previous research in Chinese. But binary is also a kind of structural relations of different discourse information in this thesis. Coordination, Subordination, and Binary can be illustrated by these three following examples.

(3.18) a. $\underline{\text{Wo}_i}$ xihuan changge,

b. $\underline{Ø_i}$ hai xihuan tiaowu.

"I like singing and dancing."

(3.19) a. $\underline{\text{Ta toufa}_i}$ hen hei,

b. $\underline{Ø_i}$ hei de xiang moshui yiyang.

"Her hair is as black as the ink."

(3.20) a. Yinwei ta shengbing,

b. suoyi ta jiu meiyou lai shangban.

"He didn't come to office, for he is sick."

The higher structure of (3.18a) and (3.18b) is Coordination, for (3.18b) moves the information of (3.18a). The higher structure of (3.19a) and (3.19b) is Subordination, for (3.19b) is just the further specification of the information of (3.19a) rather than to add new information to (3.19a). The higher structure of (3.20a) and (3.20b) is Binary, for different information which is described by (3.20a) and (3.20b) are connected by a logic relation—the causal relation.

Different information is the constituents of higher structures. The constituents in Coordination are structurally equal, in that each of the constituents in Coordination all will play their respective roles in the interpretation of the higher structure Coordination. The constituents in Subordination are structurally unequal, in that the interpretation of the higher structure Subordination is dominated by the constituent which is depended by the other constituent of Subordination. The significance of the constituents in Binary is undefined, for there are too many kinds of logic relations in Binary, and the interpretation of the higher structure Binary will be consequently decided according to the concrete logic relations.

To sum up, there are three kinds of higher structures in Chinese discourse structure: Coordination, Subordination, and Binary. Various types of higher structures are decided based on distinct ways of discourse information processing. In other words, distinct ways of discourse information processing will make the discourse information combined with different ways and then comprise different types of higher structures. Different constituents of the higher structures have distinct significance due to their distinguished roles in the interpretations of the higher structures.

#### 3.3.2.3 Parse Trees of Chinese Discourse Structure

Higher structures can be applied recursively to combine various discourse units, no matter whether discourse units are the basic units or not, until a whole discourse ensues. Concretely speaking, the basic units of a discourse are combined into large elementary units by three types of higher structures, and large elementary units are further combined into larger units with higher structures until all units of the discourse have been combined by higher structures. Hence the structure of a discourse can be built by higher structures and the basic unit of a discourse.

The discourse structure is represented as a tree which is termed the DISCOURSE PARSE TREE (DPT) in Livia (1996). The basic units of a discourse will be the leaves of the DPT, while higher structures are the nonterminal nodes of the DPT. Specifically, nonterminal nodes of the DPT will always be one of those three types of higher structures: Coordination, Subordination, or Binary, which are labeled by C, S, and B accordingly. This thesis will follow Livia's proposals. And the trees of those three types of higher structures are as follows respectively.

(3.21)

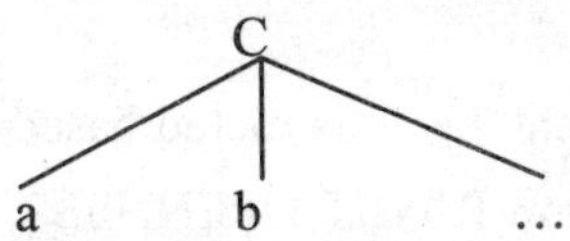


(3.22)

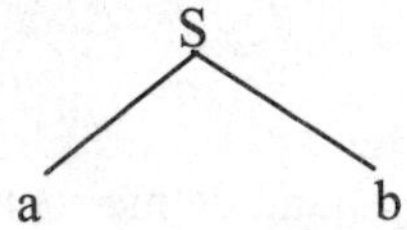


(3.23)

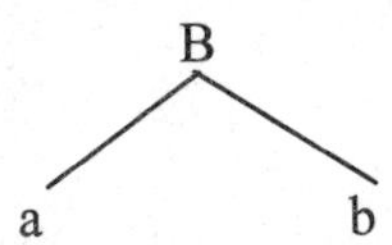


According to the above trees of higher structures, there are only two constituents in the structure Subordination and Binary except of Coordination. All constituents in Coordination are structurally equal, so there is no restriction on the quantity of the constituents of Coordination. But the constituents of Subordination and Binary are structurally unequal or undefined, and then there are only two constituents in those two kinds of higher structures.

Since Coordination, Subordination, and Binary all are decided according to distinct ways of discourse information processing, the interpretations of the nodes C, S, and B are different. The interpretation of the node C differs from its constituent, and the interpretation of the node C is the general information of all its constituents. The interpretation of the mother node S is decided by the independent constituent. Usually speaking, the left daughter of S is the independent constituent. And then the interpretation of the node S is the same as the interpretation of the left daughter, while the right daughter has no impact on the interpretation of the node S. The interpretation of the node B is another case. Both constituents of Binary have the impact on the interpretation of the node B, and hence the interpretation of the node B is the sum rather than the general information of its constituents.

There is a further restriction which constraints the power of the adjunction operation in Livia (1996). It is required that only nodes dominating the rightmost terminal of the host tree can serve as the site of the adjunction, which is called RIGHT OPENNESS in Livia (1996). Hence according to the restriction RIGHT OPENNESS, if a unit begins a new move, the previous moves become structurally unaccessible.

The parse tree of a whole discourse can be constructed based on those three types of higher structure and the restriction RIGHT OPENNESS, which can be illustrated by the following example.

(3.24) a. $\underline{\text{Niang}_i}$ zhang de jun,

b. $\underline{Ø_i}$ jun de sai guo juyuan li de xizi, qiang shang de meirenhua.

c. $\underline{\text{niang de toufa}_j}$ hei,

d. $\underline{Ø_j}$ bi mo hai hei.

e. $\underline{\text{niang de faji}_k}$ jiu you da you liang,

f. $\underline{Ø_k}$ Xiang ge bangchui xing de xian suizi.

g. $\underline{\text{niang}_i}$ xing xiao,

h. $\underline{Ø_i}$ meiyou ming.

i. nanren jiao xiangde,

j. renmen bian jiao ta xiangde nvren, xiangde laopo, xiangde jia li de, xiangde xifu.

"Mother is more beautiful than the actor in theatre and the beauty in the painting. Her hair is blacker than the ink. Her hair bun is big and round, which likes the line tassel shaped as wooden club. She has the surname Xiao, but hasn't the last name. Since the name of her husband is Xiangde, she is called Xiangde nv ren, Xiangde laopo, Xiangde jiali de, Xiangde xifu."

There are ten clauses in example (3.24). The structure of the example (3.24) can be characterized by the tree given in (3.25).

(3.25)

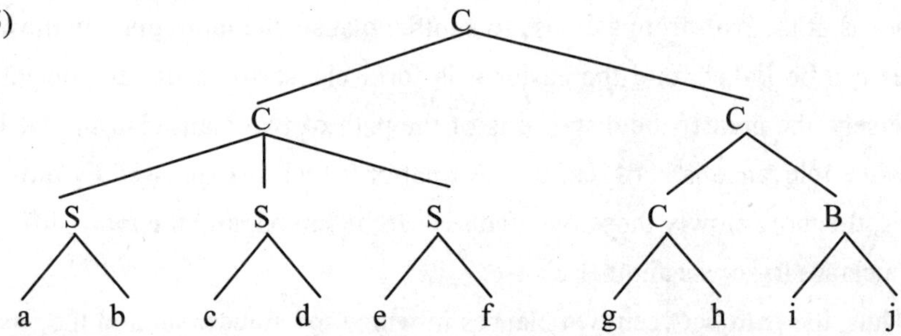


Shown in (3.25), different clauses are connected by three basic types of higher structures, and the discourse structure of a discourse can be clearly revealed by the DPT which includes all clauses of a discourse and higher structures.

## 3.3.3 How Discourse Structure Affects the Accessibility of the Antecedent

According to the discussion in 3.3.2, we can obtain a clear structure of a Chinese discourse. This part will investigate how discourse structure affects the accessibility of the antecedent.

### 3.3.3.1 Discourse Structure and the Accessibility of the Antecedent

It has been argued in the preceding text that discourse structure can affect the accessibility of the antecedent, for discourse structure or the relationship between two clauses in which the antecedent and the anaphor occur respectively could vary in different contexts and result in different accesses from the anaphor to the antecedent. Since the DPT is suggested to represent the discourse structure with a tree diagram, the impact of discourse structure on the accessibility of the antecedent can be revealed in the DPT.

The DPT is a tree which includes many different nodes which take different positions of the tree but can be connected together. Hence there is always a distinguished path between every two nodes of the DPT. Accordingly, there is a path between two clauses in which the antecedent and the anaphor occur respectively.

The path from a clause to another clause will vary with different DPTs. Some paths are near, while some are distant. Usually speaking, the shorter the distance is of the path from a clause to another clause, the more quickly those two clauses can be linked, and the easier it is for a clause to access another clause. Conversely, the greater the distance is of the path of two clauses in the DPT, the farther the relevance is between the information which is expressed by those two clauses, the more slowly those two clauses can be linked, and the more difficult it is for a clause to access another clause.

Thus, the path between two clauses in which the antecedent and the anaphor occur respectively can affect the accessibility of the antecedent by influencing the access from the anaphor to the antecedent. Generally speaking, if two clauses of the anaphora have a short hierarchical distance, they are closely relevant and the access from the anaphor to the antecedent is easy, and moreover the degree of accessibility of the antecedent is relative high. If two clauses of the anaphora have a long hierarchical distance, they are of little relevance and the access from the anaphor to the antecedent is difficult, and moreover the degree of accessibility of the antecedent is low.

The impact of the path on the accessibility of the antecedent can be illustrated by the following example.

(3.26) a. Balei wu xie xiejian de zui da aomi zaiyu shi nv yanyuan deyi yong jiaojian tiaowu de "<u>xiehe</u>$_i$".

b. "<u>xiehe</u>$_i$" cang zai xiejian li.

c. "<u>xiehe</u>$_i$" shiji shang shi yi zhong ying tao,

d. <u>Ø</u>$_i$ tao zhu jiaozhi he yi bu fen jiaomian.

e."<u>xiehe</u>$_i$" bu yong mutou, suliao, ruanmu deng cailiao,

f. <u>Ø</u>$_i$ er you 6 ceng zui putong de madaibu huo qita fangzhipin nianhe er cheng.

"The secret of ballet shoes is the 'shoe box' which can make the actress dance with the tiptoes. The 'shoe box' hides in the sharp of the shoe. It is actually a kind of the hard cover which can slip over the toes and a part of foot. The 'shoe box' is glued with six layers of the most common sackings or other textiles, rather than the wood, the plastic, or the cork."

The structure of the example (3.26) can be characterized by the tree given in (3.27).

(3.27)

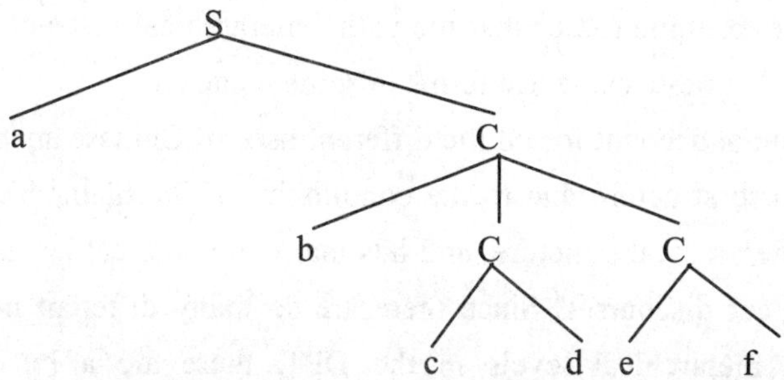


The clause (3.26b) and the clause (3.26d) have an anaphor. The noun *xiehe* in (3.26b) is the anaphor of the noun *xiehe* in (3.26a), while the zero pronoun Ø in (3.26d) is the anaphor of the noun *xiehe* in (3.26c). That is to say the anaphoric form of (3.26b) is different from that of (3.26d), though they both refer back to a same entity and they both take a same position of the clause. That difference of the anaphoric forms can be explained by the path / hierarchical distance between two clauses where the antecedent and the anaphor occur.

According to the structure represented by (3.27), the path / hierarchical distance between (3.26a) & (3.26b) is different from that between (3.26c) & (3.26d), though (3.26a & b) and (3.26c & d) both have the same linear distance. The hierarchical distance between (3.26a & b) is farther than that between (3.26c & d). As a result, the information relatedness between (3.26a & b) is different from that between (3.26c & d) in the hierarchical structure. (3.26c) and (3.26d) are related more tightly than (3.26a) and (3.26b) from the respect of the hierarchical distance. Accordingly, the access from the anaphor in (3.26d) to the antecedent in (3.26c) *xiehe* is easier than that from the anaphor in (3.26b) to the antecedent in (3.26a) *xiehe*. And the antecedent in (3.26c) *xiehe* is more highly accessible than the antecedent in (3.26a) *xiehe*. Since anaphoric forms are linguistic markers of degree of accessibility of antecedents, the anaphoric forms of (3.2b & d) should be different. The higher is the degree of accessibility of the antecedent, the less is the lexical information of the anaphoric form. As a result, the anaphoric form in (3.26d) should have less lexical information than the anaphoric form in (3.26b). The uses of anaphoric forms in example (3.26) are cxactly accordant with the above discussion: the anaphoric form in (3.26d) is the zero pronoun, while the anaphoric form in (3.26b) is the bare NP *xiehe*. It can be viewed from the example (3.26) that the path / hierarchical distance can explain different uses of Chinese anaphoric forms in some contexts.

But this cannot account for all the different uses of Chinese anaphoric forms from the discourse structure due to the complexity of the hierarchical distance. The DPT is a hierarchical structure, and has many hierarchical levels which will vary with different discourses. Since there are so many different nodes and so many different hierarchical levels in the DPT, there are a lot of different hierarchical distances between two nodes in the DPT. That is to say, the hierarchical distance between two clauses is very complicated. But not all different hierarchical distance will be clearly differentiated, because it is impossible for people's mental space to bear such a heavy memory load. Hence not all different hierarchical distance will result in different uses of Chinese anaphoric forms, which can be illustrated by the following example.

(3.28) a. <u>Dajin</u>$_i$ wang zhe niang,

b. <u>Ø</u>$_i$ jue de

c. zhe tiao nan cai de miyu haishi bu hao cai,

d. <u>Ø</u>$_i$ jiu lengzheng zhe wang zhe niang.

"Dajin is looking at the mother. He thinks it is still difficult to resolve that riddle, so he just stands and looks at the mother."

(3.29) a. <u>Ta</u>$_i$ (Ci qi'e) hui qinchi di dengdai,

b. zhidao yi zhi zugou dunshi de xiong qi'e chuxian,

c. <u>Ta</u>$_i$ caihui "fangxin'anxu".

"She (The female penguin) will reservedly wait until she finds one enough stocky male penguin, and then she will engage him silently."

The structure of the examples (3.28) and (3.29) can be characterized by the trees given by (3.30) and (3.31) respectively.

(3.30)

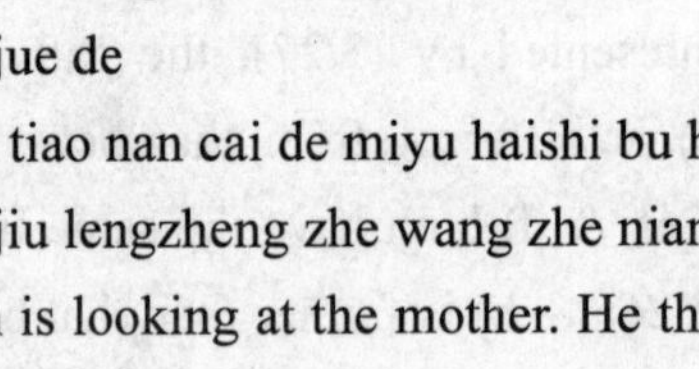

(3.31)

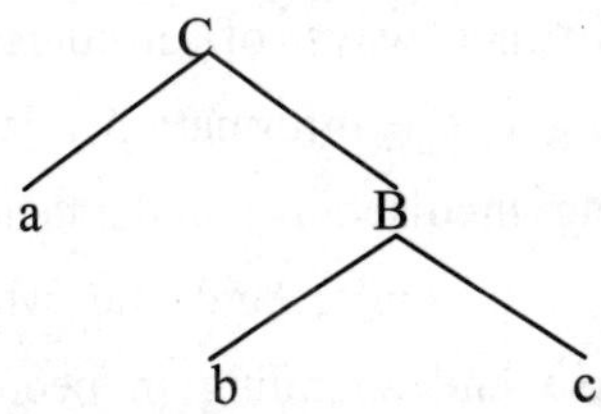


There are two different anaphoric forms in examples (3.28) and (3.29): the zero pronoun in (3.28d) which refers back to the zero pronoun in (3.28b) and the third-person pronoun *ta* in (3.29c) which refers back to the third-person pronoun *ta* in (3.29a). According to the suggestion that the hierarchical distance between two clauses in which the antecedent and the anaphor will determine the accessibility of the antecedent and further affect different uses of Chinese anaphoric forms, it is naturally expected that the hierarchical distance between (3.28b & d) is different from that between (3.28a & c) due to their different anaphoric forms. But viewed from the trees given by (3.30) and (3.31), the hierarchical distance between (3.28b & d) is the same as that between (3.28a & c): their hierarchical distances both are two nodes. Hence the hierarchical distance cannot interpret the different uses of various Chinese anaphoric forms in (3.28d) and (3.29c).

I believe that there is something else beside the hierarchical structure which should be taken into account in the interpretations of Chinese anaphoric forms, which will be discussed in the subsequent text.

#### 3.3.3.2 Three Distinct Super-node Structures Based on the DPT

It is argued in the preceding text that the DPT can explicitly reveal the structural relationship between two clauses in which the antecedent and the anaphor occur respectively. But the structural relationship between two clauses in which the antecedent and the anaphor occur respectively is not enough for the accessibility of the antecedent and the interpretations of Chinese anaphoric forms. I think that further relationship between two clauses of anaphora on information should be considered in the impact of discourse structure on the accessibility of the antecedent, in that discourse information will affect discourse understanding and anaphora understanding. Hence this part will chiefly discuss information relatedness between clauses of anaphora based on the DPT.

The DPT is just to represent distinct ways of discourse information processing. But the most important thing is the information relatedness rather than the ways of information processing in discourse understanding. When a person understands a discourse, he cannot understand the whole discourse immediately. It is because that discourse understanding in people's cognition cannot be as accurate and complicated as the DPT, in that the precise capture of the DPT needs too much inference load. Hence the reasonable interpretation on discourse understanding is that people will understand a whole discourse with a number of chunks which are related through discourse information.

This thesis argues that the information relatedness is also important for anaphora understanding. It is noted that the information relatedness is based on the universal discourse structure. The information relatedness is actually correlated with the structure closely. The discourse structure is constructed according to the generative rules. No matter how varied the discourse information is, the information connection always follows the generative rules. The same information relatedness can use many different kinds of ways of discourse information processing, while different information relatedness can be expressed with a same kind of ways of discourse information processing. So the discourse structure is the foundation of the information relatedness. And the DPT is consequently the base of the analysis of the information relatedness. Here is an example.

(3.32) a. Na shi ge ji'e de niandai.

b. daren haizi ji yi dun bao yi dun,

c. chi yecai, huaishu ye…

d. youde quanjiaren hai yuan li gutu

e. yaofan

f. qiusheng

g. qu le.

h. zai zhe jieguyan shang, Dajin taniang de nanren Xiangde de bing si le,

i. Dajin cai liang sui.

"It was an age of hunger. All people were unable to get enough to eat. They ate wild herbs, the leaves of locust tree, and others. Some families even get away from the homeland to beg for food to survive. At the critical moment, the husband of Dajin's mother Xiangde died for sick, and Dajin was just two years old."

The structure of the example (3.32) can be characterized by the tree given by (3.33).

(3.33)

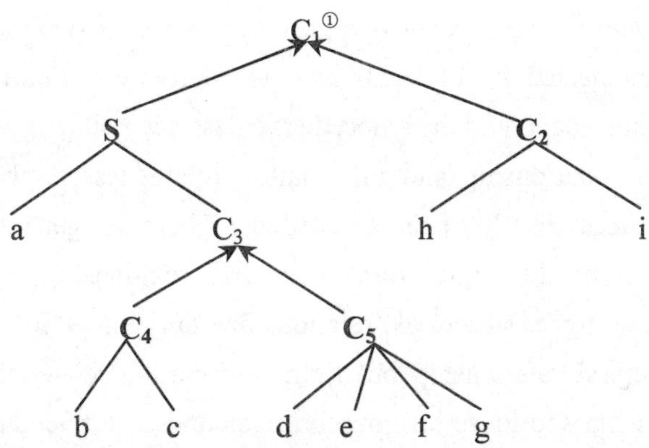


According to the tree shown in (3.33), the hierarchical distance between the node S and the node $C_2$ is the same as the hierarchical distance between the node $C_4$ and the node $C_5$, for those two pairs of nodes both are linked only by a higher structure. The node S and the node $C_2$ are linked by $C_1$, while the node $C_4$ and the node $C_5$ are linked by $C_3$. But we have different perception on the relationship between the node S and the node $C_2$ and the relationship between the node $C_4$ and the node $C_5$ from information relatedness. The information relatedness between $C_4$ and $C_5$ is tighter than that between S and $C_2$, because all clauses included by $C_4$ or by $C_5$ service for a common center/topic, while the clauses included by S differ with the clauses included by $C_2$ in the topic. As a result, the information relatedness between S and $C_2$ is different from that between $C_4$ and $C_5$. Thus, it is evident that the relationship between two nodes in the DPT can be revealed not only by the structural correlation but also by information relatedness.

Both the structural relationship and information relatedness between two clauses where the antecedent and the anaphor occur respectively can impact the

① The subscripts in the tree (3.34) are to differentiate the same kind of higher structures in different levels of the DPT.

accessibility of the antecedent. From the structural relationship, the hierarchical distance between two clauses of anaphora will affect the accessibility of the antecedent. From information relatedness, how tight two clauses of anaphora are connected will affect the accessibility of the antecedent. If two clauses of anaphora are tightly connected in information, it is easier for the anaphor to access the antecedent, and the antecedent is highly accessible. If two clauses of anaphora are loosely connected in information, it is relatively difficult for the anaphor to access the antecedent, and the antecedent is less accessible.

How the structural relationship and information relatedness between two clauses interact on the accessibility of the antecedent? There are generally four kinds of possibilities from the logic: tight structural relationship and tight information relatedness, tight structural relationship but loose information relatedness, loose structural relationship but tight information relatedness, and loose structural relationship and loose information relatedness. But actually there are three kinds of possibilities: tight structural relationship no matter what kind of information relatedness, loose structural relationship but tight information relatedness, and loose structural relationship and loose information relatedness; in that the extremely strong structural relationship between two clauses can override the effect of information relatedness so that they will be captured as a whole no matter whether there is information relatedness between them or not.

Those three kinds of possibilities are regarded as the super-node structures in this thesis and moreover termed as: Minimal Structure (MS), Local Structure (LS), and Global Structure (GS). The so-called super-node structures are beyond all nodes in the DPT, as the name suggests. There is the fundamental difference between the super-node structures and higher structures in the DPT. Higher structures are determined according to the ways of discourse information processing, and then they are purely structural. Super-node structures are mainly concerned with the information relatedness between different nodes in the DPT, and then they are semantic as well as structural.

The distinction between those three kinds of super-node structures can be illustrated more clearly from the discourse generation.

A discourse is processed clause by clause. Then when a clause is uttered, the clause takes the whole attention in people's psychological space. With the clause changing, people's attention varies. But if different clauses can be structurally linked by a kind of higher structure, they have a very tight relation due to the structural construction. As a result, those clauses can generate a kind of super-node structures in the DPT, which is the so-called MS. In other words, the MS is such a kind of super-node structure: a) the information every leave node expresses respectively is corresponding to the information expressed by a clause; and b) all information every leave node expresses respectively is immediately linked by a kind of higher structures. The MS can be represented in below.

(3.34)

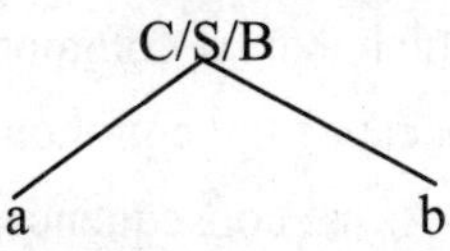


It is to be noted that the information every leave node expresses respectively is corresponding to the information expressed by a clause, rather than corresponding to a clause. That is to say, as long as the information of a node is equal to the information of a clause, that node can be a leave node of the MS. That can be illustrated by the following example.

(3.35) a. <u>Dajin</u>$_i$ wang zhe niang,

b. <u>Ø</u>$_i$ jue de

c. zhe tiao nan cai de miyu haishi bu hao cai,

d. <u>Ø</u>$_i$ jiu lengzheng zhe wang zhe niang.

"Dajin is looking at the mother. He thinks it is still difficult to resolve that riddle, so he just stands and looks at the mother."

The example (3.35) is the duplication of the example (3.28), and it can be characterized by the tree given by (3.36).

(3.36)

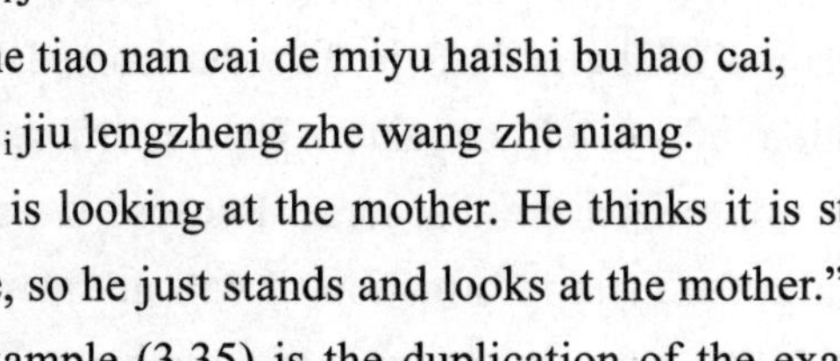


According to the tree shown by (3.36), the information of the node S isn't the information expressed by a clause. But since the interpretation of the higher structure S is totally determined by its left daughter node, the information of the node S in the tree of (3.36) is the same as the information of its left daughter node—the clause b. As a result, according to the definition of the MS in this thesis, the node S in the tree of (3.36) can still be a leave node of the MS. Thus, all nodes which are boxed off in (3.36) compose of a MS.

All nodes which are included by a MS will form a minimal segment. That minimal segment will further combine other nodes with higher structures.

Beyond the MS, the topic plays an important role on the determination of super-node structures. All the information which has a common topic can be stored together in people's working memory, because the common topic can help people memorize the different information. As a consequence, the different information which has a common topic can compose of a kind of super-node structure—the LS.

It is noted that the topic is determined by the main information of a discourse. According to the discourse structure which is discussed in 3.3.2, there is an asymmetry between different discourse information. Some discourse information is subordinated to some other discourse information. The information of the right daughter in the node S, for instance, is subordinated to the information of the left daughter, and the interpretation of the node S is thus determined by the main information—the information of its left daughter. Hence different discourse information differs in their impacts on the discourse. Because the subordinated information is subordinated to the main information, it will not play the role on the discourse information flow. As a result, the topic of the discourse information flow will not be affected by the subordinated information.

As far as the topic is concerned, there is much research on the determination of the topic. This thesis will discuss the topic in detail in the succeeding section 3.4. Here I will roughly describe the determination of the topic. The topic is actually the common information of all the main nodes in a LS.

In general, The LS can be defined as follows: a) there is at least a MS in a LS, or to say the LS is beyond the MS; and b) all main information in the LS can be linked by a common topic. The following example is such an example which is a LS.

(3.37) a. **Niang**$_i$ zhang de jun,

b. Ø$_i$ jun de

c. Ø$_i$ sai guo juyuan li de xizi, qiang shang de meirenhua.

d. **Niang de toufa**$_j$ chang,

e. xi wan tou,

f. Niang mimi de toufa$_k$ gai guo xigai,

g. Ø$_k$ xiang yi ke yu hou de chuiliur.

h. **Niang de toufa**$_l$ hei,

i. Ø$_l$ bi mo hai hei!

j. **Niang de fazan**$_m$ you da you liang,

k. Ø$_m$ xiang ge bangchui xing de xiansuizi.

"Mother is more beautiful than the actor in theatre and the beauty in the painting. Her hair is very long. Everytime she washes her hair, her long hair can screen the knee, which is like a weeping willow. Her hair is blacker than the ink. Her hair bun is big and round, which is like the line tassel shaped as wooden club."

The structure of the example (3.37) can be characterized by the tree given by (3.38).

(3.38)

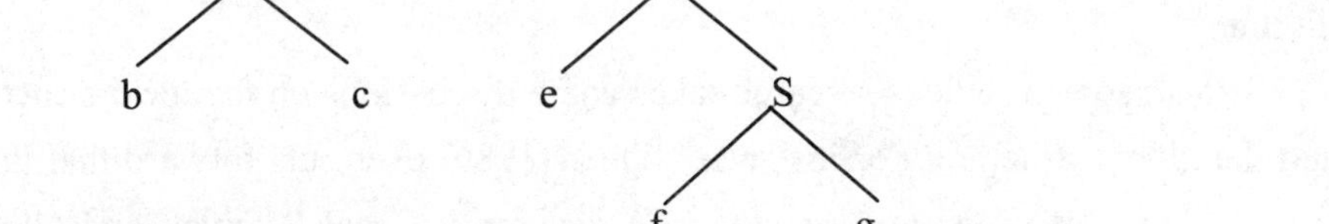


According to the tree in (3.38), there are four main nodes in the DPT: the node a, d, h, and k; which are marked bold in (3.38). Those four main nodcs have a common topic: *niang* (mother). Moreover, there are over one MS in the tree in (3.38). For instance, the node S, the node h, and the node i can establish a MS. As a consequence, two conditions of the LS have been satisfied in (3.38), and then the super-node structure of the example (3.37) is a LS.

The LS will generate a bigger segment than the MS. The bigger segment will again combine other discourse information. But as there is no common topic between different discourse information beyond the LS, the load of people's memory will become too heavy, and hence it is difficult to capture all different discourse information in short time. Such structure which is beyond the LS is so-called the Global Structure (GS). The GS can be defined as follows: the GS is such kind of the super-node structures which is beyond the LS.

To sum up, there are three kinds of super-node structures based on the DPT: the MS, the LS, and the GS.

The MS is only concerned with the information in people's attention space. There is a very close relatedness between the information in the MS due to all information can be linked by a node of the higher structure. But there is no special requirement on the topic relatedness of all nodes in a MS.

There is the structural variability in the LS, and we thus cannot link all the information through the structures. But the topic plays an important role in the LS. If there is a common topic between different information, it is easy for people to link different information. Hence there is a requirement that all clauses in a LS have to be linked by a common topic.

And there is the structural as well as the semantic variability in the GS, and all nodes are linked by a more general topic or have no topic relatedness in a GS. Thus, it is hard to link so much information in a short period of the time.

The MS, the LS, and the GS can clearly distinguish three distinct levels of a discourse.

In fact some previous research takes some discussions on the local structure and the global structure. For instance, Sidner (1986) ever puts forward that there are two kinds of different segments in a discourse: Local Segment and Global Segment. It is argued in Sidner (1986) that a discourse can be segmentalized according to different intentions in which each intention can produce a local structure and generate a discourse segment which is composed of many utterances. Smith (2003) is also the study based on the local structure of a discourse: there are different patterns of various local segments of discourses. It can be seen from the previous research that most research agrees that there are two kinds of different levels in a discourses: local structure and global structure. The local structure will be tighter than the global structure semantically. But the distinction between the local structure and the global structure is too general in the previous research, which is not conducive to further study. Thus, this thesis re-analyzes the structure of a discourse, and proposes three kinds of super-node structures based on the further distinction from the information relatedness of the DPT: the Minimal Structure (MS), the Local Structure (LS), and the Global Structure (GS).

There is another interesting correspondence on discourse levels between the proposal in this thesis and that in the traditional Chinese discourse research. There is little research on Chinese discourse structure. But there is a prevailing view on Chinese discourse levels in the traditional Chinese linguistics; that is there are two kinds of levels in a Chinese discourse based on the basic unit the *sentence*: the discourse paragraph and the whole discourse. This thesis argues that there are three discourse levels based on the basic unit the *clause*: the MS, the LS, and the GS. It seems that the view on Chinese discourse levels in this thesis is different from that in the traditional Chinese linguistics. But in fact there is the similarity between those two views in some contexts, in which some sentences are actually equivalent with the MS and some discourse paragraphs can be analyzed as the LS.

In general, the previous research can just provide a good evidence for the distinction between the MS, the LS, and the GS in this thesis. And moreover, the distinction between the MS, the LS, and the GS is reasonable and appropriate to be applied to take the further study on discourse phenomena in Chinese.

#### 3.3.3.3 The Impact of Super-node Structures on the Accessibility of the Antecedent

Three kinds of super-node structures have different impacts on the accessibility of the antecedent.

In the MS, all information of the leave nodes is linked by only one higher structure. Hence the different information in the MS is highly accessible due to the extremely strong structural relationship. In respect of anaphora, if the anaphora occurs in a MS, it is very easy for an anaphor to access its antecedent in a MS, and consequently the degree of accessibility of the antecedent is very high.

But in the LS, the access from the anaphor to the antecedent will be relatively difficult than that in the MS. The following two reasons can account for the difference: a) the hierarchical distance between two clauses in the LS is definitely farther than that in the MS; and b) all information in the LS is linked only by one common topic. As a result, the access from the anaphor to the antecedent will be more difficult than that in the MS. But since there is a common topic in all information of the LS, the access between two clauses is still relatively easy.

The access from the anaphor to the antecedent in the GS is naturally very difficult, in that there is no structural as well as information relatedness between two clauses in the GS. And thus it will take a long time for people to access the antecedent from the anaphor.

In general, three kinds of super-node structures, the MS, the LS, and the GS, can affect the access from the anaphor to the antecedent, and will thus affect the accessibility of the antecedent. The correlation between super-node structures and the accessibility of the antecedent is illustrated by the following table.

**Table 3.1 Super-node Structures and the Accessibility of the antecedent**

| The Accessibility of the Antecedent | Super-node Structures Where Anaphora Occurs |
|---|---|
| Highest | Minimal Structure |
| Middle | Local Structure |
| Lowest | Global Structure |

This thesis will chiefly analyze the impact of discourse structure on the interpretations of Chinese anaphoric forms based on the impacts of those three kinds of super-node structures on the accessibility of the antecedent.

## 3.4 Topicality and the Accessibility of the Antecedent

It is argued in the preceding text that topicality will affect the accessibility of the antecedent, and it will thus affect uses of Chinese anaphoric forms. So this section will analyze how the topicality affects the accessibility of the antecedent.

### 3.4.1 Some Previous Discussions on Topicality

The topicality chiefly discusses the status of an entity being a topic or not. There are many discussions on the notion ***topic*** in the literatures. Some research analyzes the topic from the syntactic or semantic perspective, say Aissen (1992), Xu and Liu (2003), Xu and Liu (2007), Hu and Pan (2001), and Shi (2000). Some analyzes the topic from the discourse perspective, say Grosz et al. (1995), Hu and Pan (2002), and Cui (2004). Since Chinese anaphora is a kind of discourse phenomena, this thesis will mainly analyze the topic from the discourse perspective.

Generally speaking, there are two main questions on the topic: a) what is the definition of the topic; and b) how many kinds of topics there are in a discourse. Those two questions are entangled between each other.

The *topic* is often defined in terms of the aboutness or the givenness in some literatures. The aboutness refers to what a discourse/discourse segment/clause is about. And the givenness refers to the given information of a discourse/discourse segment/clause. Aissen (1992) cite the aboutness as a central feature of the topic. And Reinhart (1983) also argues that the topic is primarily what a sentence is about, and that givenness is neither a sufficient nor necessary condition for topicality.

Centering Theory (CT) defines the topic from a new perspective. It proposes that the topic refers to the center of attentional state of a speaker/hearer (Cf. Grosz et al. (1986, 1995), Beaver (2002), Hu and Pan (2002), and Cui (2004), etc.). In Grosz et al. (1995), discourse entities fall into two kinds of centers:

*backward-looking centers* ($C_b$) and *forward-looking centers* ($C_f$). $C_b$ is the center of the current utterance①, while $C_f$ is ranked for the potential/possible centers of the next utterance.

Beaver (2002) makes a terminological change: *topic* instead of *backward-looking center*. Ward (1988) even suggests the identification of those two notions. But there is little difference between the topic and the backward-looking center according to their determination. Beaver (2002) argues that the *topic* of a sentence is the entity referred to in both the current and the previous sentence, such that the relevant entity in the previous sentence was minimally oblique. If there is no such entity, the topic is undefined.

In general, the topic is defined either through the aboutness of a unit or through the relevant entities between different units in the previous research. The view that the topic is defined based on the aboutness of a unit is too general, and the topic is thus hard to be defined. In contrast, that the topic is defined through the relevant entities between different units is easier to operate relatively.

Besides the definition of the topic, there are many discussions on the types of the topic in the previous research, which includes two questions. One is there are how many topics in a clause, one topic or more than one topic, and the other is whether there is any other kind of topics besides the topic of a clause.

It is widely accepted that the clause, or the basic unit of a discourse, has its own topic. But how many topics there are in a clause results in many discussions. Some research argues that each clause has at most one topic, whereas some research argues that each clause can have two or more topics. CT, for instance, suggests each utterance has at most one topic. But Beaver (2002) has a different view. Beaver (2002) divides the *topic* into different kinds: UNIQUE TOPIC and SALIENT TOPIC, which is defined in (3.39) and (3.40).

(3.39) UNIQUE TOPIC With respect to any sentence, there is exactly one discourse entity which is the topic of that sentence.

(3.40) SALIENT TOPIC The topic of a sentence is the most salient discourse

① In Centering Theory, the basic element for discourse analysis is **utterance**. But in this thesis, **clause** is the basic element for discourse analysis. And the definition of **clause** in this thesis will be discussed in last section about discourse structure.

entity referred to in that sentence, and undefined if no previously salient entities are referred to.

Roughly speaking, the distinction between Unique Topic and Salient Topic chiefly pays attention to the quantity of relevant entities between two connective sentences in Beaver (2002): one or more. If there is only one entity of a sentence which is relevant with the previous sentence, it is the unique topic of the sentence. If there is more than one relevant entity, there are many topics of the sentence such that the topics in the sentence can be further distinguished according to their saliency.

In some other literatures, a clause/sentence could have more than one topic in which the topics can be differentiated as main topic and sub-topic, the big topic and the small topic, the first topic and the second topic, and so on (Cf. Lu (1979), Huang and Liao (1997)).

Besides the discussion on the topics of a clause/sentence, some literatures argue that there is a kind of topic which differs with the topic in a clause/sentence.

Hu and Pan (2002) put forward a notion *discourse segment topic* (DST). They argue that DST is necessary and $C_b$[①] should be distinguished from DST in Chinese discourses, in that there is a division of labour between $C_b$ and DST. $C_b$ is used to track the focus of a sentence, whereas DST is used to track the focus of a discourse segment. When $C_b$ plays a role in defining transition states, DST will not play a role in making a discourse segment coherent. However, when $C_b$ does not play a role in case there is no $C_b$, DST will play a major role in making the discourse coherent. As a consequence, Hu and Pan (2002) argue that the establishment of DST is different from that of $C_b$. DST belongs to the discourse segment, whereas $C_b$ belongs to the sentence. When DST is identified in a discourse segment, it will not change within the same discourse segment. However, $C_b$ needs to be identified in every sentence and it may change from sentence to sentence. Therefore the $C_b$ should be determined for each sentence, and the DST does not need to be determined for each sentence. Once the DST is

① $C_b$ is usually regarded as the topic of a clause/sentence.

chosen, it will only be checked that whether there is DST shift in the analysis. As to the definition of $C_b$, Hu and Pan (2002) restrict $C_b(U_i)$ to be the element in $C_f(U_{i-1})$ that is realized by the subject pronoun or the pronoun contained in the subject in $U_i$. And their definition on DST is as follows.

> *The first DST is chosen by pronouns or related elements in the second sentence $U_2$. If there is more than one pronoun or related element in $U_2$, then the antecedent of the higher ranked one is chosen as the DST. If there is no pronoun or related element in $U_2$ or the antecedent is not in $U_1$, then choose the subject of $U_1$ as the DST.*

Katz (1980) also involves discourse topic. He proposes that "the surface-subject position imposes the rhetorical or stylistic role of DISCOURSE TOPIC on an NP occupying it, especially one that has been moved into that position… The notion of a discourse topic is that of the common theme of the previous sentences in the discourse, the topic carried from sentence to sentence as the subject of their predications."

In all, the term "topic" has been used diversely in the previous research. I will subsequently give my own definition on the topic, and further try to find out how the topicality of the antecedent and the anaphor affects the accessibility of the antecedent.

### 3.4.2 Determining of the Topic

According to the above discussion, it is obvious that there are three main questions on the topic: a) how many kinds of topics there are in Chinese discourses; b) if there are more than one kind of topics in Chinese discourses, how to define each kind of topics; and c) how many topics there are in a clause.

As to the first question, how many kinds of topics there are in Chinese discourses, I propose that there are two kinds of different topics in Chinese discourses which should be distinguished: one is the topic of a clause, and the other is the topic of a discourse segment.

When a clause of a discourse is uttered, the clause is in people's attentional state. There is always a focus of people's attentional state. As a consequence, every clause of a discourse will have a focus. The focus of a clause is actually the topic of the clause.

But in some contexts, a couple of clauses have a common concerned entity, no matter what is the topic of each clause. Therefore the common concerned entity is the focus of those clauses, and moreover can make those clauses be combined into a discourse segment through information relatedness. Naturally the common concerned entity is the topic of the discourse segment. Since the discourse segment which is determined by information relatedness is termed the Local Structure in this thesis, the topic of a discourse segment is the topic of a LS.

Both the topic of a clause and the topic of a LS are necessary in discourse understanding, for those two kinds of topics exist in different discourse levels and play different roles in a discourse.

Now let's come to the second question: how to define each kind of topics. The *topic* is usually defined in terms of aboutness or the focus/center of the attentional state in the previous research. The aboutness and the focus of the attentional state both can reveal some features of the topic. But they catch different features of topics, which can be illustrated by the following example.

(3.41) a. Women de xuexiao zuoluo zai jingse youmei de xiao he pang.

b. Zou jin da tie men,

c. shouxian zhanxian zai yanqian de shi conglv de shang caochang,

d. shang caochang de zhongjian shi yi tiao bizhi de da dao fenge nanbei,

e. dao pang liang bian shi liang pai bu gao de pingguo hua.

f. da dao de nan mian zaizhong le ji pai maomi de songbai,

g. touguo ta ke yixi kan dao yanying zhong de xin jiaogong sushe,

h. houmian haiyou xushuichi.

i. da dao de bei mian you ji ke gaoda de changqingshu yu luoyeshu xiangjian,

j. ce suo duocang zai zhe da shu xia ye xiande you ji fen touqi.

"Our school is at the side of a beautiful river. There is a playground at the front of the mental gate. The middle of the playground is a straight road which divides the south and the north. At the both sides of that road are two lines of low apple-blossoms. In the south of the road grow several lines of thick conifers through which we can see the new teachers' apartments. There is a reservoir in the back of the conifers. In the north of the road are some large evergreen trees and deciduous trees. There is a toilet under the tree which seems more ventilated."

There are ten clauses in the above example (3.41). And the aboutness of those ten clauses is *women DE xuexiao* (our school). But the focuses of the attentional state of those ten clauses vary. The focus of attentional state in (3.41a) is *women DE xuexiao* (our school). As the discourse unfolds, the focus of the attentional state shifts from *da tie men* (a big iron door), *shang caochang* (ascending playground), *shang caochang DE zhongjian* (the middle of ascending playground), *dao pang*(side of road), *da dao DE nanmian*(south of road), *songbai* (a kind of tree), *houmian* (the back), *da dao DE beimian* (north of road), to *zhe da shu* (that big tree) in (3.41b-j) in turn.

So it can be seen from example (3.41) that the aboutness can be unchanging, the focus of the attentional state varies, however. That indicates that the focus of the attentional state is more subjective to change than the aboutness. The focus of the speaker/hearer's attentional state can update clause by clause, while the aboutness can hold for some clauses. As a result, I think, the aboutness is more appropriate to be used to describe the topic of a LS, while the focus of the attentional state is more appropriate to be used to describe the topic of a clause. Admittedly, the aboutness of a clause is the same with the focus of the attentional state in some contexts, but not in all contexts.

In general, the topic of a clause is the focus of the attention state, whereas the topic of a LS is the aboutness of all clauses in the LS. The focus of the attentional state has ever been discussed in CT. So this thesis will take the definition of $C_b$ in GJW 95 as a reference, and define the *topic* of a clause as follow.

(3.42) the Determination of **the Topic of a Clause**

*The* ***topic*** *of a clause is the entity occurred in both the current and the previous clauses. If there is no realized entity from the previous clause, the topic of the current clause is the subject of the clause.*

As to the topic of the LS, its determination differs from the topic of a clause naturally. It can be seen from the preceding discussion that, roughly speaking, the topic of a LS is the common concerned entity of all clauses of the LS. But it is noted that the dependant clauses of a LS will not affect the determination on the topic of a LS, in that they just serve for the independent clauses and will not impact the discourse information flow. The right daughter of the node S, for instance, is dependant / subordinated to the left daughter of the node S. The interpretation of the node S is totally determined by the left daughter. So it is evident that the information which is dependant / subordinated to some other information will not affect the whole discourse information flow. And the independent / subordinated information thus cannot affect the topic of the LS. Hence the topic of a LS should be determined based on the relevance of the entities which occur in the independent clauses realized as main nodes in the DPT. The detail definition of the topic of the LS is as follows.

(3.43) the Determination of **the Topic of a LS**

*If there is a related entity between all connective main nodes which are beyond the MS, those main nodes and the subordinated nodes included by them belong to a LS and the related entity is the topic of the LS. If there is more than one related entity between different connective main nodes, the higher ranked one or the most related entity from the information perspective in the first main node is the topic of the LS.*

*If there is only a main node as well as some subordinated nodes in a discourse, in which there is at least a MS, the main node and the subordinated nodes can establish a LS. The highest ranked entity of the first main node will be chosen as the topic of the LS.*

It is obvious that there are two main different constructions to the LS. There are many main nodes in some LS, while there is only a main node in some LSs. Here is an example on the topic of a LS.

(3.44) a. **Niang**$_i$ zhang de jun,

b. Ø$_i$ jun de sai guo juyuan li de xizi, qiang shang de meirenhua.

c. **Niang** de toufa$_j$ chang,

d. xi wan tou,

e. Niang mimi de toufa$_k$ gai guo xigai,

f. Ø$_k$ xiang yi ke yu hou de chuiliur.

g. **Niang de toufa**$_l$ hei,

h. Ø$_l$ bi mo hai hei!

i. **Niang de faji**$_m$ you da you liang,

j. Ø$_m$ xiang ge bangchui xing de xiansuizi.

"Mother is more beautiful than the actor in theatre and the beauty in the painting. Her hair is very long. Everytime she washes her hair, her long hair can screen the knee, which is like a weeping willow. Her hair is blacker than the ink. Her hair bun is big and round, which is like the line tassel shaped as wooden club."

The structure of the example (3.44) can be characterized by the tree given by (3.45).

(3.45)

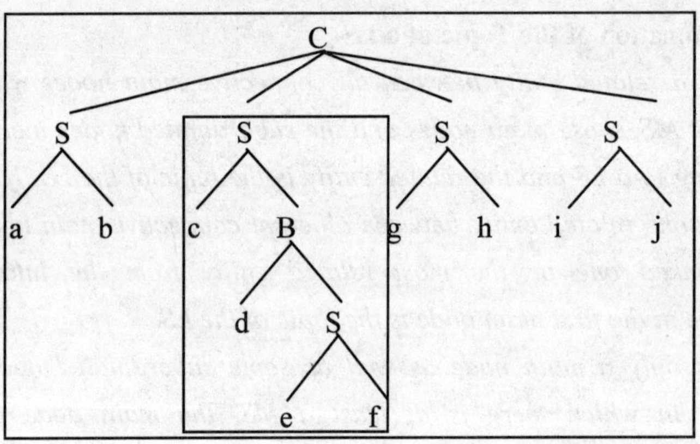


There are two LSs in example (3.44). One is the LS including the clauses c, d, e, and f, and the other is the LS including all clauses in example (3.44).

Let us look at the LS including the clauses c, d, e, and f firstly. The node of the clause c is a main node, for it is the left daughter of the node S. The node of the clause d is subordinated to the node of the clause c. Since the nodes c and d cannot be constrained by a MS, they compose of a LS. Moreover, the highest ranked entity of the clause c, *niang de toufa* (mother's hair), is the topic of the LS.

As to the nodes a and c, they both are the main nodes of the DPT. Moreover, both the node a and the node c are beyond the MS, and they should thus compose of a LS. For the same reason, the nodes g and i can be also taken into account. In other words, the nodes a, c, g, and i compose of a LS. The topic of the LS should be the related entity of those clauses. Hence we can obtain the topic of the LS: *niang* (the mother).

It can be seen from the above example that we can determine the topic of the LS based on the relevant entities and the significance of the nodes.

Generally speaking, there are two kinds of topics which should be distinguished in Chinese discourses: the topic of a clause and the topic of the LS.

Now come to the final question herein: how many topics in a clause. According to the above definition of the topic of a clause, each clause will at least have one topic. Some clauses will have two or more topics. Here are some examples.

(3.46) Beijing shijian 12 yue 21 ri 3 shi 30 fen (Yidali dangdi shijian 20 ri 20 shi 30 fen)， yijia di shisi lun kaishi di 2 chang juezhu.

"The second game of Serie A Week 14 began at 3:30 on December 21 of Beijing time (20:30 on December 20 of Italian time)."

(3.47)a. Shijie daxuesheng yundonghui jintian chansheng 26 mei jinpai,

b. Zhongguo xuanshou duode qizhong 3 kuai.

c. Eluosi daibiaotuan pingjie zai yishu ticao xiangmu shang de chuse fahui,

d. jintian gong huode 8 kuai jinpai.

"There are 26 golden medals today on the Universiade. Chinese athletes have won 3 golden medals. And Russian delegation has won 8 golden medals today by virtue of the excellent performance in Rhythmic Gymnastics."

(3.48)a. You ge chang huai guan'ai zhi xin de shenshi$_i$ zou jin yi jia huadian,

b. Ø$_i$ yaoqiu ba chuchuang li de hua qu chu yibufen,

c. dian li de ren$_j$ zhao zhe ta$_i$ de hua qu zuo,

d. Ø$_j$ bing wen ta$_i$ yao mai duoshao.

"A gentleman, who is always caring others, came into a flower shop and asked to take a part of flowers out of the show window. The shop assistant did like what he told and asked how many flowers he wanted to buy."

In example (3.46), the clause is the first clause of a discourse. Then there is no previous clause, and subsequently there is no entity of the previous clause which can be realized in the current clause. So the topic of the current clause in (3.46) is the subject *yijia di shisi lun* (14th round of Italian Serie A).

In example (3.47), none of the clauses are the initial clause of a discourse, but not all two connective clauses will have the relevant entity. There are no relevant entities between (3.47a) and (3.47b) as well as between (3.47b) and (3.47c). Therefore the topics of (3.47a-c) are the subjects of (3.47a-c) respectively.

There are four clauses in (3.48). There is an entity which occurs in all clauses of the example (3.48). That entity is *shenshi* (gentleman). As a consequence, that entity is the topic of (3.48a-d). Moreover, there is another topic in (3.48d), for the entity *dian li de ren* occurs in (3.48c) as well as in (3.48d). And the entity *dian li de ren* is consequently a topic of the clause (3.48c).

It can be seen that a clause has at least one topic, in that there is always a focus in people's attentional state.

To sum up, there are two kinds of topics in Chinese discourses: the topic of a clause and the topic of a LS. Those two kinds of topics both are determined by the focus of people's cognition. Furthermore, a clause can have more than one topic, whereas a LS has only one topic.

### 3.4.3 The Topicality and the Accessibility of the Antecedent

The above discussion on the topic is to prepare for the analysis of the topicality on the accessibility of the antecedent. I argue, whether the antecedent and the anaphor are the topic or not will affect the access from the anaphor to the antecedent and further impact the accessibility of the antecedent.

Most of the previous research on anaphora only considers whether the antecedent rather than the anaphor is a topic or not, in that it proposes that only the antecedent can affect the degree of accessibility of the antecedent (Cf. Givón (1983), Ariel (1990), Y. Xu (2004), etc.). But I argue the antecedent and the anaphor both can affect the degree of accessibility of the antecedent, for both the antecedent and the anaphor can affect the access from the anaphor to the antecedent. Typically, if the antecedent or the anaphor is the topic, they are highly accessible in people's cognition and it is easy for people to access the antecedent from the anaphor, and the degree of accessibility of the antecedent is consequently high. Otherwise, the degree of accessibility of the antecedent is relatively low. Thus, the topicality of the antecedent and the anaphor can affect the accessibility of the antecedent due to their different behaviors on the topicality.

Moreover, I make a distinction between two types of topics in this thesis: the topic from the clause and the topic from a larger discourse segment. Those two kinds of topics play the role in different super-node structures and can affect the behaviors of the antecedent and the anaphor based on their topicality.

In a MS, there is only the topic of the clause. Since the topic of a clause will update clause by clause, the antecedent and the anaphor are not required to be consistent on the topic of a clause. Therefore there are four different kinds of behaviors / four patterns of the antecedent and the anaphor in a MS from the perspective of the topicality: both the antecedent and the anaphor are the topic; the antecedent is the topic of a clause, whereas the anaphor isn't; the antecedent isn't the topic of a clause, whereas the anaphor is; or neither the antecedent nor the anaphor is the topic.

But in a LS, the topic of a discourse segment rather than the topic of a clause is the main concern. The antecedent and the anaphor in a LS are always consistent with the topic of the LS, for the topic of a LS will hold from the first clause to the last clause of the LS. Concretely speaking, if the antecedent is the topic of the LS in which the antecedent occurs, the anaphor is, too; and vice versa.

In a GS, whether the antecedent and the anaphor is the topic of a LS rather than the topic of a clause will be considered from the perspective of the topicality, in that only the topic of a LS will be paid attention to beyond the LS. Since the topic of a LS will differ from that of different LSs, the antecedent and the anaphor will not be required to be consistent with each other in the topic. Hence there are also four patterns of the antecedent and the anaphor in a GS from the topicality.

Overall, there are various patterns of the antecedent and the anaphor in different super-node structures based on whether the antecedent and the anaphor are the topic or not. Different patterns of Chinese anaphora based on whether the antecedent and the anaphor are the topic or not will result in different degree of accessibility of the antecedent through the impact on the access from the anaphor to the antecedent. The detail corresponding relation between the patterns of the antecedent and the anaphor on the topicality and the accessibility of the antecedent is shown below.

(3.49) the Correspondence between the Topicality and the Accessibility of the Antecedent

a) If the antecedent and the anaphor both occur in a MS, there are four different patterns of the antecedent and the anaphor on the topicality.

**Table 3.2 The Topicality and the Accessibility of the Antecedent in a MS**

| The degree of accessibility of the antecedent | The antecedent is the topic of a clause | The anaphor is the topic of a clause |
|---|---|---|
| Highest | + | + |
| Middle | + | - |
| | - | + |
| Lowest | - | - |

b) If the antecedent and the anaphor both occur beyond a MS but in a LS, there are two patterns of the antecedent and the anaphor on the topicality.

**Table 3.3 The Topicality and the Accessibility of the Antecedent in a LS**

| The degree of accessibility of the antecedent | The antecedent is the topic of a LS | The anaphor is the topic of a LS |
|---|---|---|
| High | + | + |
| Low | - | - |

c) If the antecedent and the anaphor both occur in a GS, there are four different patterns of the antecedent and the anaphor on the topicality.

**Table 3.4 The Topicality and the Accessibility of the Antecedent in a GS**

| The degree of accessibility of the antecedent | The antecedent is the topic of a LS | The anaphor is the topic of a LS |
|---|---|---|
| Highest | + | + |
| Middle | + | - |
| | - | + |
| Lowest | - | - |

According to (3.49), there are different degrees of accessibility of the antecedent as the antecedent and the anaphor vary in the topicality. The correlation in (3.49) will be further used to analyze the impact of the topicality on the interpretations of Chinese anaphoric forms, because it has clearly revealed the impact of the topicality on the accessibility of the antecedent.

## 3.5 Saliency and Accessibility of the Antecedent

This section will firstly mention some discussions on the saliency, and subsequently propose the determination of the saliency, and finally discuss how the saliency affects the accessibility of the antecedent.

### 3.5.1 Some Discussions on Saliency

Much previous research has discussed the saliency of an entity which has been variably termed "salience", "saliency", or "cognitive saliency" in the literature. This thesis uses "saliency" for our purposes. There are three main questions widely discussed: a) how to determine the saliency of an entity, b) the relation between the saliency and the form, and c) the saliency change.

Most papers propose that the saliency of an entity is determined by its grammatical role, such as GJW95, Jiang (2004), Wang (2006), and so on. In GJW 95, the ranking of all entities of an utterance is according to the saliency of the entities. And moreover the saliency of all entities of an utterance is chiefly determined by their grammatical roles: SUBJECT > DIRECT OBJECT > INDIRECT OBJECT > OTHERS. Beaver (2002) proposes that the saliency of an entity is determined by its grammatical obliqueness. The grammatical obliqueness is being used as a practical operationalization of the saliency, or the psychologists might term activation. The subject of an utterance is usually viewed as the mostly activated entity among all entities of the utterance. Other entities of the utterance which take other positions all are oblique to the entity taking the subject position from the activation. That is to say the activation of the entities of an utterance is actually determined by their positions. As a result, that the saliency of an entity is determined by its grammatical role is the same as that the saliency of an entity is determined by its grammatical obliqueness.

The determination of the saliency of an entity is relatively simple. Besides that, it is also argued that there is a relation between the saliency and the form in the previous research. For example, it has been suggested that for Japanese, NPs marked (by the choice of main verb) as empathetic are highly salient, and that wa-marked NPs are even more salient (Cf. Kuno (1987), Walker et al. (1994), etc.). Similarly, it has been suggested initially for German by Strube and Hahn (1999), and then for English by Strube (1998), that the form of an entity in the previous sentence is a better predictor of the saliency than its argument position. Beaver (2002) also proposes that there is some relation between the saliency① and the form and further gives a definition on SALIENT FORM which is shown below.

(3.50) SALIENT FORM If in the previous sentence discourse entity α was realized by a more minimal form than discourse entity β, then α is more salient than β.

The general proposal on the relation between the saliency and the form is that the form of an entity will be more minimal with its saliency strengthening or that the form of an entity can mark some degree of the saliency. Actually the previous research on the saliency also indicates that there is a close relation between the saliency and anaphoric forms. Since this thesis argues that the saliency isn't the only factor which will affect the uses of Chinese anaphoric forms, this thesis will not study the relation between the saliency and the anaphoric form, but the relation between those four factors and Chinese anaphoric forms.

Besides the correlation between the saliency and the form, the saliency of an entity will vary with contexts. Beaver (2002) puts forward a rule RECENCY to represent the saliency change.

(3.51) RECENCY One discourse entity is more salient than another if the first was referred to in a later clause.

① Beaver (2002) uses the term 'salience'.

Such a rule captures the idea that saliency declines over time, which can benefit the treatments of a variety of anaphora phenomena such as intrasentential anaphora, longer distance anaphora, and so on. (Cf. Grosz and Sidner (1986), Hitzeman and Poesio (1998))

There is less research about the saliency of an entity in Chinese than that in English. The saliency of an entity in Chinese is mostly regarded as determined by the grammatical roles, which is the same with the treatment of English. But Cui (2004) argues that only grammatical roles can not control the saliency of entities in Chinese. Cui (2004) proposes that the saliency of entities in Chinese is determined by the givenness as well as the grammatical role, and moreover the givenness plays a more important role in determining the saliency than the grammatical role.

In general, the previous research mainly pays attention to the determination of the saliency of entities and the relation between the saliency and the form.

### 3.5.2 The Determination of the Saliency

As mentioned above, there are two main proposals on the determination of the saliency of entities. One is the saliency of an entity is determined by its grammatical roles or its grammatical obliqueness. And the other is the saliency of an entity is determined by its givenness status and its grammatical role. The main controversy between those two kinds of proposals on the saliency is whether the givenness can affect the saliency of an entity or not.

As mentioned in the previous text, the givenness status of an entity is twined with its status on the topicality. For instance, if an entity is a topic, it is usually given. And this thesis will thus adopt the first proposal; that is to determine the saliency of an entity according to its grammatical role in a clause: SUBJECT > DIRECT OBJECT > INDIRECT OBJECT > OTHERS, based on which the impact of the saliency on the accessibility of the antecedent will be further analyzed.

### 3.5.3 The Saliency and the Accessibility of the Antecedent

The notion *saliency* in this thesis refers to the saliency in people's cognition.

Generally speaking, the more salient an entity is, the easier it is for people to catch. As far as Chinese anaphora is concerned, if an antecedent and its anaphor are more salient, both of them will be more easily captured, and then the access from the anaphor to the antecedent is easier, hence the antecedent is highly accessible. Otherwise, if an antecedent and its anaphor are less salient, both of them will not be easily captured, and then the access from the anaphor to the antecedent is difficult, hence the antecedent is lowly accessible. Thus, the saliency of the antecedent and the anaphor can affect the degree of accessibility of the antecedent.

The saliency of an entity will vary with its grammatical role in a clause. There is huge difference between the most salient entity and the entities which are not most salient, in that the most salient entity always can arouse the particular attention in people's cognition. As a result, this thesis will mainly consider whether the antecedent and the anaphor are the most salient entities or not when analyzing the impact of the saliency on the accessibility of the antecedent.

According to whether the antecedent and the anaphor is the most salient in their occurring clauses, we can obtain four patterns of the antecedent and the anaphor: a) both the antecedent and the anaphor are the most salient, b) the antecedent is the most salient while the anaphor isn't, c) the anaphor is the most salient while the antecedent isn't, and d) neither the antecedent nor the anaphor is the most salient. Those four patterns of Chinese anaphora will result in different degrees of accessibility of the antecedent due to the impact of the saliency on the accessibility of the antecedent, which are given below.

**Table 3.5　The Impact of the Saliency on The Accessibility of the Antecedent**

| The degree of accessibility of the antecedent | The antecedent is the most salient entity of a clause | The anaphor is the most salient entity of a clause |
|---|---|---|
| Highest | + | + |
| Middle | + | - |
| | - | + |
| Lowest | - | - |

According to Table 3.5, the accessibility degree of the antecedent will vary with the saliency of antecedent and anaphor. When the antecedent and the anaphor are the most salient in their occurring clauses, the accessibility degree of the antecedent is highest.

When the antecedent or the anaphor is not the most salient in a clause, it will increase the inference load from the anaphor to the antecedent. There are two patterns in which the antecedent or the anaphor is not the most salient. One pattern is the saliency increase between the antecedent and the anaphor, and the other pattern is the saliency decay between the antecedent and the anaphor. But no matter which pattern, they both will increase the inference load from the anaphor to the antecedent. And consequently the degree of accessibility of the antecedent in those two patterns is lower than that in the pattern where the antecedent and the anaphor both are the most salient.

When an antecedent and its anaphor both are not the most salient, the inference load from the anaphor to the antecedent is heaviest. Therefore the degree of accessibility of the antecedent is lowest from the saliency.

In general, whether the antecedent or the anaphor is the most salient will affect the degree of accessibility of the antecedent, which is shown in Table 3.5. This thesis will analyze the impact of the saliency on uses of Chinese anaphoric forms based on the correlation in Table 3.5.

## 3.6 Referential Distance and the Accessibility of the Antecedent

The factor of referential distance between the antecedent and the anaphor is relatively simple. There are a variety of referential distances between the antecedent and the anaphor in different contexts. But only whether the antecedent is most recent for the anaphor or not will be considered in this thesis, because the capture of many entities in a discourse relies more on the hierarchical structure or information relatedness rather than the linear structure, so only the most recent antecedent will be prominent in people's cognition and consequently is easy for the anaphor to access.

According to whether the antecedent occurs in a preceding connective clause for the anaphor, there are two patterns of the antecedent and the anaphor from referential distance: a) the antecedent occurs in a preceding connective clause for the anaphor, and b) the antecedent doesn't.

Accordingly, those two patterns will result in two kinds of different degrees of accessibility of the antecedent. If the antecedent occurs in a preceding connective clause for the anaphor, it is recent for the anaphor in people's cognitive status, and the anaphor can easily access the antecedent, and hence the antecedent is more accessible for the anaphor. Otherwise, the antecedent is less accessible. As a result, the antecedent which is recent has a higher degree of accessibility than that which isn't recent. The correlation between those two patterns of the antecedent and the anaphor and the accessibility of the antecedent is given by Table 3.6.

**Table 3.6 The Impact of Referential Distance on the Accessibility of the Antecedent**

| The degree of accessibility of the antecedent | the antecedent occurs in a preceding connective clause for the anaphor |
|---|---|
| Highest | + |
| Lowest | - |

According to Table 3.6, from the perspective of referential distance, the degree of accessibility of the antecedent is highest given the antecedent occurs in a preceding connective clause for the anaphor; otherwise the degree of accessibility of the antecedent is lowest.

## 3.7 Interpreting the Uses of Chinese Anaphoric Forms

As mentioned in the preceding text, there are two aspects in interpretations of Chinese anaphoric forms: what factors and how the factors will affect uses of Chinese anaphoric forms. Since this thesis will study Chinese anaphoric forms based on the accessibility which views anaphoric forms as linguistic markers of degrees of accessibility of antecedents, those two aspects in interpretations of Chinese anaphoric forms are actually as follows: a) what factors can affect the accessibility degree of the antecedent in Chinese, and b) how those factors affect the accessibility degree of the antecedent and further affect uses of Chinese anaphoric forms.

The preceding text has proposed that four main factors can affect the accessibility of the antecedent and has revealed the respective impacts of those four main factors on the accessibility of the antecedent, which provides a solid foundation for the interpretations on the uses of various Chinese anaphoric forms. The section will mainly analyze how to combine the respective impacts of those four main factors into a whole and determine the accessibility of all kinds of antecedents, and moreover try to correlate different antecedents with different degrees of accessibility to different Chinese anaphoric forms. Hence the distinctive uses of Chinese anaphoric forms are expected to be interpreted.

### 3.7.1 Two Difficulties and the Resolutions

Various anaphoric forms are differently used in Chinese discourses. But their distinctive uses have not been clearly revealed in the previous research. The main reason is, in my opinion, that the previous research has not resolved two difficulties in the interpretations on the uses of Chinese anaphoric forms.

#### 3.7.1.1 The Ranking of Antecedents on the Accessibility

The first difficulty is that different antecedents with distinguished degrees of accessibility have not been rightly identified in the previous research such that the correlation between different antecedents and anaphoric forms cannot be rightly obtained.

As mentioned above, there are four main factors which can affect the accessibility of the antecedent. How those four factors together determine the accessibility of the antecedent? The ideal status is to combine the respective impacts of those four factors on the accessibility of the antecedent, and then find out a clear order of different degrees of antecedents. However it is much complicated to rank precisely different degrees of accessibility of antecedents.

The accessibility is a cognitive status so that it is hard to determine the precise impacts of different factors on the accessibility of the antecedent. As a consequence, it is very difficult to rank different degrees of accessibility of antecedents which are resulted from different impacts of different factors. For instance, will the case that the antecedent is most salient make the antecedent more accessible than the case that the antecedent is recent? It is hard to tell. Hence different degrees of accessibility of antecedents are difficult to rank by simply combining all different impacts of the main factors on the accessibility. And accordingly different antecedents with different degrees of accessibility are difficult to rank in the previous research.

Thus, unlike the treatments of the previous research on the accessibility of the antecedent, this thesis will not integrate all factors into a whole to rank the accessibility of different antecedents, but will categorize four main factors into two groups which can interact in determining the accessibility of antecedents and ranking different degrees of accessibility.

Concretely speaking, the four main factors which can affect the accessibility of the antecedent will be grouped into two parts: one is the impact of discourse structure, and the other is the general impact of topicality, saliency, and referential distance. It is because there is a huge difference between those two kinds of impacts on the accessibility of the antecedent. Discourse structure affects the accessibility of the antecedent from two clauses where the antecedent and the anaphor occur respectively, while other three factors all affect the accessibility of the antecedent from the antecedent and the anaphor by changing some behaviors of the antecedent and the anaphor. Thus, this thesis will separately analyze the impact of discourse structure and the general impact of topicality, saliency, and referential distance, and further discuss the interaction between them and try to find out the overall impact of four main factors on the accessibility of the antecedent. Such kind of the research can refrain from the precise determination on the effect of different factors on the accessibility of the antecedent, and at the same time can rightly judge the accessibility of different antecedents through the above interaction. As a result, different antecedents could be clearly ranked on the accessibility, which is necessary for the interpretations on the uses of Chinese anaphoric forms.

#### 3.7.1.2 The Mismatch between the Accessibility of Antecedents and Anaphoric Forms

The second difficulty of the interpretations on the uses of Chinese anaphoric forms is that there is a mismatch between the accessibility of the antecedent and Chinese anaphoric forms.

Logically speaking, each variation of the antecedent and the anaphor on discourse structure, topicality, saliency, and referential distance can affect the accessibility of the antecedent and consequently result in different degrees of accessibility of the antecedent. Those different kinds of variations of the antecedent and the anaphor can be integrated and generate a total of 96 different degrees of accessibility of the antecedent based on the preceding discussion of this thesis.

But there are only four main types of Chinese anaphoric forms: the zero pronouns, the overt pronouns (the third-person pronoun *ta* and the definite pronoun *zhe*/ *na*), descriptive NPs, and full NPs.

It is obvious that there is a big mismatch between the accessibility of the antecedent and Chinese anaphoric forms. How to solve the mismatch?

In fact, it is impossible to use different anaphoric forms to mark all different degrees of accessibility of the antecedent. As there are a lot of different degrees of accessibility of the antecedent, if every subtle change of accessibility degree will cause the essential impact on people's cognition, people's inference load will be too heavy. That is evidently illogical. The reasonable interpretation about the relation between the accessibility degree of the antecedent and the anaphoric form is that not all degrees of accessibility of the antecedent require different Chinese anaphoric forms to encode, but some similar degrees of accessibility of the antecedent are marked by one type of Chinese anaphoric forms.

That can be more explicitly described through the continuum of the degree of accessibility of the antecedent. I suggest that all different degrees of accessibility of the antecedent can establish a continuum, which is so-called the accessibility continuum of the antecedent. There are two poles in the accessibility continuum: the highest accessibility of the antecedent and the lowest accessibility of the antecedent.

But not every degree of accessibility of antecedents will require a distinct kind of anaphoric forms to encode it, for some different but similar degrees of accessibility of antecedents have the same cognitive status. Therefore all degrees of accessibility of antecedents should be reduced into four distinguished domains, which range different spans on the accessibility continuum of the antecedent. Those four distinguished domains will result in the essential impact on people's cognitive status, and they consequently require different kinds of Chinese anaphoric forms.

Moreover, the highest degree of accessibility of the antecedent is special. When the antecedent is most accessible for the anaphor, the anaphora can make the discourse most coherent and consequently is most preferred due to the economy in language using. Hence the highest degree of accessibility of the antecedent can exert the essential impact in people's cognitive status, and should be encoded by a distinctive type of Chinese anaphoric forms. As a result, it constitutes a distinguished domain of the accessibility continuum, which should be encoded by the simplest anaphoric forms- the zero pronouns.

Except the highest degree of accessibility of the antecedent, other degrees of accessibility will not be so prominent in people's cognitive status, and will consequently not require a distinctive type of Chinese anaphoric forms to encode. As a consequence, among other degrees other than highest degree of accessibility of the antecedent, some different but similar degrees of accessibility will form a distinguished domain of the accessibility continuum which requires a type of anaphoric form to encode. Here is the correspondence between the distinguished domains of the accessibility continuum of the antecedent and Chinese anaphoric forms.[①]

① ZP, OPs, DesNPs, and FNs are to express the zero pronoun, the overt pronouns (the third-person pronoun *ta* and definite pronouns *zhe/na*), descriptive NPs, and full NPs respectively in the figures and the tables hereafter.

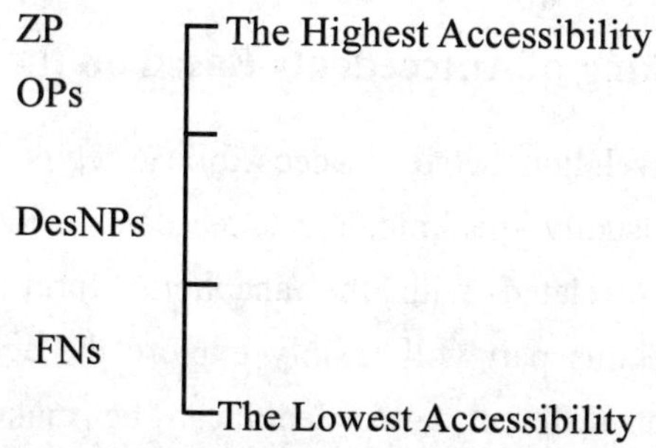


**Fig. 3.2 The Representation of Chinese anaphoric forms on the Accessibility Continuum of the Antecedent**

The above proposal that there are some distinguished domains of the accessibility continuum of the antecedent can well solve the mismatch between Chinese anaphoric forms and different degrees of accessibility of the antecedent. Hence this thesis will interpret Chinese anaphoric forms based on the proposal.

More concretely speaking, this thesis will reduce all kinds of degrees of accessibility of antecedents and further attempt to distinguish several kinds of antecedents which have distinctive degrees of accessibility between each other; based on which those several kinds of antecedents will be ranked on the accessibility and be further related to anaphoric forms.

#### 3.7.1.3 General Resolutions

In general, these two aspects are important for the interpretations on uses of Chinese anaphoric forms.

Firstly, different impacts of different factors on the accessibility of the antecedent cannot be mixed into a whole, which will make some antecedents with different degrees of accessibility difficult to be recognized and differentiated. This thesis further proposes that the impacts of four main factors on the accessibility of the antecedent should be firstly classified into two groups due to different impact ranges: one is the impact of discourse structures, and the other is the general impact of topicality, saliency, and referential distance.

And secondly, some different but similar degrees of accessibility of antecedents should be regarded as a general but distinctive group which requires the same kind of Chinese anaphoric forms to encode.

### 3.7.2 The Ranking of Antecedents Based on the Accessibility

There is a correlation between accessibility degree of the antecedent and anaphoric forms. Usually speaking, the antecedents with the higher degree of accessibility are correlated with the anaphoric form with less descriptive information. Hence this part will mainly explore the accessibility of different antecedents so that different antecedents can be ranked according to their accessibility, which prepares for the interpretations on the uses of Chinese anaphoric forms.

As mentioned above, the impact of discourse structure and the impacts of topicality, saliency, and referential distance should be separately discussed. As a consequence, this part will firstly analyze the impact of discourse structure on the ranking of antecedents through the accessibility, and secondly explore the general impact of topicality, saliency, and referential distance on the ranking of antecedents, and finally attempt to give an overall ranking of all kinds of antecedents.

#### 3.7.2.1 Discourse Structure and the Ranking of Antecedents

This thesis has suggested that discourse structure is a necessary factor which can affect the accessibility of the antecedent. Moreover, this thesis poses that discourse structure chiefly affects the accessibility of the antecedent through the super-node structures.

There are three distinct kinds of super-node structures in Chinese discourses according to the analysis of this thesis: the Minimal Structure, the Local Structure, and the Global Structure. There is a huge difference between different super-node structures on the relations between different clauses. In the MS, different clauses are tightly connected due to a common higher structure. In the LS, there is no tight structural relation but a common topic between different clauses, and different clauses are consequently not connected so tightly as those in the MS. In the GS, there is no tight structural relation as well as no common topic between different clauses, and the clauses are thus connected loosely.

The relation between two clauses in which the antecedent and the anaphor occur respectively can naturally affect the accessible relation between them, in that the accessible relation between the antecedent and the anaphor is always captured based on the understanding of two clauses where the antecedent and the anaphor occur respectively. As a result, the accessibility of the antecedent will vary with super-node structures.

The tighter are two clauses where the antecedent and the anaphor occur respectively from the structural relationship and information relatedness, the more accessible the antecedent is highly accessible for the anaphor. Thus, if the anaphora occurs in a MS, the antecedent should be more accessible for the anaphor than that of the anaphora which occurs in a LS or a GS. For the same reason, the antecedent of the anaphora which occurs in a LS should be more accessible for the anaphor than that of the anaphora which occurs in a GS. And hence the ranking order of antecedents on the accessibility based on discourse structure can be obtained: the Antecedents in the MS > the Antecedents in the LS > the Antecedents in the GS.

It can be indicated from the above discussion that the super-node structures actually give a partition on all kinds of antecedents. Precisely speaking, all kinds of antecedents are classified into three sets: one set includes the antecedents in a MS, one set includes the antecedents in a LS, and one set includes the antecedents in a GS. Those three sets of antecedents vary in the accessibility due to the impact of super-node structures on the accessibility, and they are consequently ranked differently.

#### 3.7.2.2 Topicality, Saliency, and Referential Distance and the Ranking of Antecedents

The topicality, the saliency, and referential distance are other three main factors which can affect the accessibility of the antecedent. Their respective effect on the accessibility of the antecedent has been discussed in the preceding text in detail. Briefly speaking, these behaviors of the antecedent and the anaphor will result in different accessibility of the antecedent: whether the antecedent or the anaphor is a topic, whether the antecedent or the anaphor is most salient, and whether the antecedent and the anaphor occur in two connective clauses. How to integrate the above impacts into a whole and give an overall ranking on different antecedents?

In my opinion, since the antecedent and the anaphor both denote a same discourse referent, various behaviors of the antecedent and the anaphor on topicality, saliency, and referential distance actually reflect the change of a discourse referent on those three factors in discourse information flow. Different kinds of change of a discourse referent will differently impact people's cognitive status, and the accessibility of the antecedent is consequently different. As a result, the behaviors of the antecedent and those of the anaphor on topicality, saliency, and referential distance should be both considered in analyzing the impact of topicality, saliency, and referential distance on the accessibility of the antecedent. That is to say this thesis will mainly analyze the pair of the antecedent and the anaphor (AN-pair hereafter), based on which different degrees of accessibility of the antecedent are expected to achieve.

Based on the above discussion, this thesis will firstly analyze the behaviors of the antecedents and those of the anaphors on topicality, saliency, and referential distance and their impacts on the accessibility of the antecedent respectively, and secondly analyze the integrated behaviors of the pair of the antecedent and the anaphor on them which can result in different degrees of accessibility of the antecedent.

**3.7.2.2.1 The Behaviors of Antecedents and the Accessibility of Antecedents**

The behaviors of the antecedent on topicality, saliency, and referential distance are not too complex. Briefly speaking, these aspects of the antecedent will result in different degrees of accessibility of the antecedent: whether the antecedent is a topic, whether the antecedent is most salient, and whether the antecedent occurs in a preceding connective clause. Those three kinds of aspects of the antecedents on topicality, saliency, and referential distance are labeled as [±T], [±S], and [±C] respectively.

Each variations of the antecedent in those three kinds of aspects can result in the change of cognitive status, and consequently render different degrees of accessibility. Concretely speaking, the respective behaviors of antecedents on topicality, saliency, and referential distance—[±T], [±S], and [±C]—can be further combined, based on which there are eight different antecedents with different behaviors on topicality, saliency, and referential distance: [+T, +S, +C],

[+T, +S, -C], [+T, -S, +C], [+T, -S, -C], [-T, +S, +C], [-T, -S, +C], [-T, +S, -C], and [-T, -S, -C]. Naturally those eight kinds of different behaviors of antecedents will lead to eight kinds of degrees of accessibility. And then those eight kinds of antecedents can be further ranked based on the degrees of accessibility.

In order to give a clear ranking order on those eight kinds of antecedents, we take a close look at the impact of topicality, saliency, and referential distance on the accessibility of the antecedent. I argue that the impacts of topicality, saliency, and referential distance on the accessibility of the antecedent are distinctive in people's cognitive status. The topicality is concerned with the information flow of a discourse, which is very important in discourse understanding. The saliency only pays attention to the current cognitive status of discourse entities. And referential distance is just related to the recency of discourse entities. Hence it can be indicated that the topicality can affect the accessibility of the antecedent more greatly than the saliency and referential distance.

As far as the saliency and referential distance are concerned, they just affect the accessibility of the antecedent slightly based on the impact of the topicality. Moreover, referential distance can affect the accessibility of the antecedent a bit greatly than the saliency, in that the recency involves something about discourse information flow while the saliency only focuses the state of entities in a clause. Hence the recency plays a more important role for discourse phenomenon than the saliency.

Based on the above discussions, the above eight kinds of antecedents can be ranked into such an order on the accessibility: [+T, +S, +C] > [+T, -S, +C] > [+T, +S, -C] > [+T, -S, -C] > [-T, +S, +C] > [-T, -S, +C] > [-T, +S, -C] > [-T, -S, -C]. The antecedents that occur in more left of the ranking order are more accessible.

#### 3.7.2.2.2 The Behaviors of Anaphors and the Accessibility of Antecedents

As mentioned in the preceding text, the behaviors of the anaphor in topicality and saliency can also affect the accessibility of the antecedent, in that those behaviors of the anaphor can affect the access from the anaphor to the antecedent. Take an antecedent with [+T, +S, +C] for example. The antecedent with [+T, +S, +C] is always most accessible of those eight kinds of antecedents. But with the anaphor changing in topicality and saliency, the specific degree of accessibility of the antecedent with [+T, +S, +C] can also vary. The anaphor in the subject position, for instance, can more easily access the antecedent with [+T, +S, +C] than the anaphor in the object position due to the saliency of the anaphor, in that the former anaphor can make the discourse more coherent than the latter one. Hence the anaphor should also be taken into account in analyzing the accessibility of the antecedent.

There are only two kinds of behaviors of the anaphors which can affect the accessibility of the antecedent on topicality, saliency, and referential distance: a) whether the anaphor is a topic, which is labeled as [±T], and b) whether the anaphor is most salient, which is labeled as [±S]. Those behaviors of anaphors can be combined and form four kinds of anaphors from the topicality and the saliency: [+T, +S], [+T, -S], [-T, +S], and [-T, -S].

Those four kinds of anaphors can also result in different degrees of the antecedent, in that different kinds of anaphors can make the capture of the antecedents different. The ranking order of the antecedent on accessibility rendered by the behaviors of the anaphor on topicality and saliency is as follows: [+T, +S] > [+T, -S] > [-T, +S] > [-T, -S], for the topicality can affect the accessibility of the antecedent more greatly than the saliency.

#### 3.7.2.2.3 The Pairs of the Antecedent and the Anaphor and the Ranking of Antecedents

Different behaviors of the antecedent and those of the anaphor on topicality, saliency, and referential distance can be further combined, which are the pairs of the antecedent and the anaphor. Different pairs of the antecedent and the anaphor can actually result in different degrees of accessibility of the antecedent due to different impacts of the antecedent and the anaphor on the accessibility of the antecedent. As a result, different antecedents can be ranked on the accessibility from the pairs of the antecedent and the anaphor on topicality, saliency, and referential distance.

According to the discussions in 3.7.2.2.1 and 3.7.2.2.2, there are eight kinds of behaviors of the antecedent and four kinds of behaviors of the anaphor on topicality, saliency, and referential distance. Different kinds of the antecedent and those of the anaphor can be combined. As a consequence, there are four kinds of anaphor as to each kind of the antecedent; and there are eight kinds of the antecedent as to each kind of the anaphor. Hence there are totally 32 kinds of pairs of the antecedent and the anaphor, which is shown with number below.

**Table 3.7 The pairs of the Antecedent and the Anaphor**

| | [+T,+S] | [+T,-S] | [-T,+S] | [-T,-S] |
|---|---|---|---|---|
| [+T,+S,+C] | 1 | 2 | 3 | 4 |
| [+T,-S,+C] | 5 | 6 | 7 | 8 |
| [+T,+S,-C] | 9 | 10 | 11 | 12 |
| [+T,-S,-C] | 13 | 14 | 15 | 16 |
| [-T,+S,+C] | 17 | 18 | 19 | 20 |
| [-T,-S,+C] | 21 | 22 | 23 | 24 |
| [-T,+S,-C] | 25 | 26 | 27 | 28 |
| [-T,-S,-C] | 29 | 30 | 31 | 32 |

Different pairs of the antecedent and the anaphor will render different degrees of accessibility of the antecedent and further affect the uses of Chinese anaphoric forms, as different AN-pairs will lead to various inference loads in discourse understanding. The ideal status of anaphora is to make discourse most coherent, which requires the antecedent and the anaphor both are topics, the most salient, and connective. In other words, when the antecedent is [+T, +S, +C] and the anaphor is [+T, +S], the inference load from the anaphor to the antecedent is lightest. As a consequence, the antecedent in that kind of the AN-pairs is most accessible and should be encoded by the simplest anaphoric form. But some anaphora cannot keep the antecedent and the anaphor positive in topicality, saliency, and referential distance. In such kinds of the AN-pairs, the inference load from the anaphor to the antecedent will increase, and different degree of accessibility of the antecedent occurs.

In general, different kinds of the pairs of the antecedent and the anaphor can result in different degrees of accessibility of the antecedent through the impact on the inference load from the anaphor to the antecedent and discourse coherence, which will further affect the uses of Chinese anaphoric forms.

There are a total of 32 kinds of the AN-pairs, and there are consequently 32 different degrees of accessibility of antecedents. But not all kinds of different degrees of accessibility of the antecedent will require different anaphoric forms, in that there is always the fuzziness in people's cognition and some similar degrees of accessibility of the antecedent will be encoded by the same anaphoric form.

I argue that the impact of the topicality on the accessibility of the antecedent is much greater than those of the saliency and referential distance, because the topicality is concerned with the information flow of a discourse and is very important in discourse understanding. The saliency only pays attention to the current cognitive status of discourse entities. And referential distance is just related to the recency of discourse entities. Hence we can firstly differentiate the AN-pairs based on the different behaviors of the antecedent and the anaphor on the topicality.

Three distinctive types of pairs of the antecedent and the anaphor can be obtained according to the behaviors of the antecedent and the anaphor on the topicality: **Continuation** when both the antecedent and the anaphor are the topics; **Shift** when only one of the antecedent and the anaphor is the topic; and **Link** when neither the antecedent nor the anaphor is the topic. The detail distributions of those three types of pairs of the antecedent and the anaphor are illustrated below.

**Table 3.8 Three types of pairs of the Antecedent and the Anaphor based on the Topicality**

| | [+T,+S] | [+T,-S] | [-T,+S] | [-T,-S] |
|---|---|---|---|---|
| [+T,+S,+C] | Continuation | Continuation | Shift | Shift |
| [+T,-S,+C] | Continuation | Continuation | Shift | Shift |
| [+T,+S,-C] | Continuation | Continuation | Shift | Shift |
| [+T,-S,-C] | Continuation | Continuation | Shift | Shift |
| [-T,+S,+C] | Shift | Shift | Link | Link |
| [-T,-S,+C] | Shift | Shift | Link | Link |
| [-T,+S,-C] | Shift | Shift | Link | Link |
| [-T,-S,-C] | Shift | Shift | Link | Link |

It is no doubt that those three types of the pairs of the antecedent and the anaphor—the Continuation, the Shift, and the Link—will differently affect the accessibility of the antecedent. Obviously, the antecedents in the Continuation will be more accessible for the anaphor than the antecedents in the Shift, in that the entities which are the topics are always more prominent in people's cognition than those which are not the topics. For the same reason, the antecedents in the Shift will be more accessible for the anaphor than the antecedents in the Link. As a result, all kinds of antecedents can be classified into three sub-sets from the topicality, the saliency, and referential distance: one sub-set includes the antecedents in Continuation, one includes the antecedents in Shift, and one includes the antecedents in Shift. Moreover, those three sub-sets of antecedents can be ranked into such a ranking order on the accessibility: the antecedents in Continuation > the antecedents in the Shift > the antecedents in the Link. The more left is the AN-pair in the ranking order, the more highly accessible is the antecedent for the anaphor.

It is to be observed that those three types of the AN-pairs could be further refined according to the behaviors of the antecedent and the anaphor on the saliency and referential distance. But as the impacts of the saliency and referential distance on the accessibility of the antecedent are much less, some impacts will be overridden by the impacts of the topicality and discourse structure for the interpretations of Chinese anaphoric forms. Hence it is not necessary to analyze the effects of the saliency and referential distance on the AN-pairs as detail as possible. This thesis will analyze the impact of the saliency and referential distance on uses of Chinese anaphoric forms in the interaction of discourse structure and the AN-pairs.

#### 3.7.2.3 The Overall Ranking of Antecedents

Discourse structure, topicality, saliency, and referential distance are four main factors which can affect the accessibility of the antecedent. Moreover, those four main factors are grouped into two categories: one is discourse structure and the other is the topicality, the saliency, and referent distance, duc to their huge difference on the impact on thc accessibility of the antecedent. Discourse structure chiefly affects the accessibility of the antecedent through three kinds of super-node structures, while the topicality, saliency, and referential distance mainly affect the accessibility of the antecedent through different AN-pairs. This part will mainly study how those two categories interact on affecting the accessibility of the antecedent.

I think the chief idea in the interaction between discourse structure and the AN-pairs on the accessibility of the antecedent is that the same AN-pairs may result in different degrees of accessibility of the antecedent in different kinds of super-node structures. This thesis argues that discourse structure can greatly affect the accessibility of the antecedent through three different kinds of super-node structures—the MS, the LS, and the GS, while the topicality, the saliency, and referential distance affect the accessibility of the antecedent through different kinds of the AN-pairs. Since different kinds of the AN-pairs can occur in different super-node structures, the degrees of accessibility of the antecedent, rendered by different kinds of the AN-pairs, will further vary with the super-node structures. More precisely speaking, the super-node structures can categorize all kinds of antecedents into three sets, and the AN-pairs can further classify those three sets of antecedents into more sub-sets of antecedents which are closely related with the uses of Chinese anaphoric forms.

Thus, this thesis will combine the super-node structures and the AN-pairs to analyze the uses of Chinese anaphoric forms.

#### 3.7.2.3.1 The Pairs of the Antecedent and the Anaphor in the MS

There are totally 32 kinds of the AN-pairs according to the logic, which are further classified into three kinds: the Continuation, the Shift, and the Link. In fact some logical pairs of the antecedent and the anaphor are not allowed in the MS due to the definition of the topic of a clause which is repeated below.

(3.52) The **topic** of a clause is the entity occurred in both the current and the previous clauses. If there is no realized entity from the previous clause, the topic of the current clause is the subject of the clause.

According to the above definition of a topic of a clause, the AN-pairs in which the antecedent is [+C] while the anaphor is [-T] cannot occur. As a consequence, there are 8 kinds of impossible AN-pairs and 24 kinds of possible AN-pairs in the MS, which is given in Table 3.9.

**Table 3.9 The Possible Pairs of the Antecedent and the Anaphor in the MS**

| | [+T,+S] | [+T,-S] | [-T,+S] | [-T,-S] |
|---|---|---|---|---|
| [+T,+S,+C] | Continuation | Continuation | * | * |
| [+T,-S,+C] | Continuation | Continuation | * | * |
| [+T,+S,-C] | Continuation | Continuation | Shift | Shift |
| [+T,-S,-C] | Continuation | Continuation | Shift | Shift |
| [-T,+S,+C] | Shift | Shift | * | * |
| [-T,-S,+C] | Shift | Shift | * | * |
| [-T,+S,-C] | Shift | Shift | Link | Link |
| [-T,-S,-C] | Shift | Shift | Link | Link |

It can be viewed from Table 3.9 that some Shift AN-pairs and some Link AN-pairs have been prohibited in the MS. But there are still three kinds of AN-pairs—the Continuation, the Shift, and the Link.

As indicated in the preceding text, the saliency and referential distance can further refine those three kinds of AN-pairs. In fact, different super-node structures can affect the refinement of the saliency and referential distance. Generally speaking, the effects of the saliency and referential distance on the accessibility of the antecedent will be more sensitive in the MS than those in the LS or the GS, because the great lowering of the LS or the GS on the accessibility of the antecedent will compress the effects of other factors into a small corner in people's cognition. As a result, the concrete impacts of the saliency and referential distance on the accessibility of the antecedent may differ in different super-node structures.

I argue that the Continuation can be sub-classified into Strong Continuation and Weak Continuation in the MS. When both the antecedent and the anaphor are positive on the saliency and referential distance, the AN-pair is **Strong Continuation**, for the topicality, the saliency, and referential distance will not lower the accessibility of the antecedent. When either the antecedent or the anaphor is negative on the saliency and referential distance, the AN-pair is **Weak Continuation**, for the change on the saliency and referential distance will result in a special attention in people's cognitive status and make the antecedent not so accessible for the anaphor.

In the Continuation AN-pairs, the impact of saliency is the same with that of referential distance. But in the Shift and Link AN-pairs, the impact of referential distance is more significant than that of the saliency in the MS, in that the role of the recency is greater than the role of the grammatical functions in the capture of the entities which are not the topics. The Shift AN-pairs and the Link AN-pairs both include the entities which are not the topics. As a result, those two kinds of the AN-pairs can be further sub-classified according to the change on referential distance. In the Shift AN-pairs, when the antecedent is [+C], the Shift AN-pairs are Smooth Shift; otherwise the Shift AN-pairs are Rough Shift. In the Link AN-pairs, when the antecedent is [+C], the Link AN-pairs are Short Link; otherwise the Link AN-pairs are Distant Link. The detail AN-pairs in the MS can be illustrated in the table below.

**Table 3.10　The Pairs of the Antecedent and the Anaphor in the MS**

| | [+T,+S] | [+T,-S] | [-T,+S] | [-T,-S] |
|---|---|---|---|---|
| [+T,+S,+C] | Strong Continuation | Weak Continuation | * | * |
| [+T,-S,+C] | Weak Continuation | Weak Continuation | * | * |
| [+T,+S,-C] | Weak Continuation | Weak Continuation | Rough Shift | Rough Shift |
| [+T,-S,-C] | Weak Continuation | Weak Continuation | Rough Shift | Rough Shift |
| [-T,+S,+C] | Smooth Shift | Smooth Shift | * | * |
| [-T,-S,+C] | Smooth Shift | Smooth Shift | * | * |
| [-T,+S,-C] | Rough Shift | Rough Shift | Distant Link | Distant Link |
| [-T,-S,-C] | Rough Shift | Rough Shift | Distant Link | Distant Link |

It can be viewed from Table 3.10 that there is no Short Link in the MS due to restriction of the topic of a clause.

In general, there are five kinds of AN-pairs in the MS: Strong Continuation, Weak Continuation, Smooth Shift, Rough Shift, and Distant Link.

#### 3.7.2.3.2　The Pairs of the Antecedent and the Anaphor in the LS

32 kinds of logical AN-pairs will greatly reduce in the LS, in that only the topic of the LS is concerned with in the LS. The topic of a LS will not change in the LS, so there is no Shift AN-pair in the LS. There are only 16 kinds of possible

AN-pairs in the LS which are shown below.

**Table 3.11 The Possible Pairs of the Antecedent and the Anaphor in the LS**

| | [+T,+S] | [+T,-S] | [-T,+S] | [-T,-S] |
|---|---|---|---|---|
| [+T,+S,+C] | Continuation | Continuation | * | * |
| [+T,-S,+C] | Continuation | Continuation | * | * |
| [+T,+S,-C] | Continuation | Continuation | * | * |
| [+T,-S,-C] | Continuation | Continuation | * | * |
| [-T,+S,+C] | * | * | Link | Link |
| [-T,-S,+C] | * | * | Link | Link |
| [-T,+S,-C] | * | * | Link | Link |
| [-T,-S,-C] | * | * | Link | Link |

The saliency and referential distance can also further sub-classify the Continuation and the Link AN-pairs in the LS into two kinds: Strong Continuation and Weak Continuation, Short Link and Distant Link.

But the differentiation between Strong Continuation and Weak Continuation in the LS is different from that in the MS. In the LS, the role the topic plays on discourse understanding is so great while the roles of the saliency and referential distance are less. Hence, in the Continuation AN-pairs of the LS, if there is no more than one negative variation of the antecedent or the anaphor on the saliency or referential distance, the Continuation AN-pairs is Strong Continuation; and other Continuation AN-pairs are Weak Continuation.

The difference between Short Link and Distant Link in the LS is the same with that in the MS. As long as the antecedent is [+C], the Link AN-pairs are Short Link; otherwise the Link AN-pairs are Distant Link.

The detailed AN-pairs in the LS can be illustrated below.

**Table 3.12 The Pairs of the Antecedent and the Anaphor in the LS**

| | [+T,+S] | [+T,-S] | [-T,+S] | [-T,-S] |
|---|---|---|---|---|
| [+T,+S,+C] | Strong Continuation | Strong Continuation | * | * |
| [+T,-S,+C] | Strong Continuation | Weak Continuation | * | * |
| [+T,+S,-C] | Strong Continuation | Weak Continuation | * | * |

| | [+T,+S] | [+T,-S] | [-T,+S] | [-T,-S] |
|---|---|---|---|---|
| [+T,-S,-C] | Weak Continuation | Weak Continuation | * | * |
| [-T,+S,+C] | * | * | Short Link | Short Link |
| [-T,-S,+C] | * | * | Short Link | Short Link |
| [-T,+S,-C] | * | * | Distant Link | Distant Link |
| [-T,-S,-C] | * | * | Distant Link | Distant Link |

In total, there are four kinds of AN-pairs in the LS: Strong Continuation, Weak Continuation, Short Link, and Distant Link.

#### 3.7.2.3.3 The Pairs of the Antecedent and the Anaphor in the GS

There is no reduction on the logical AN-pairs in the GS. Therefore there are 32 kinds of different AN-pairs in the GS. And the Continuation, Shift, and Link AN-pairs can also be sub-classified into six kinds: Strong Continuation and Weak Continuation, Smooth Shift and Rough Shift, and Short Link and Distant Link. But the detailed differentiations of different AN-pairs in the GS are different from those in the MS and those in the LS.

The role of the topicality has been greatly weakened in the GS, because there is no strong connection on the topic in a GS. Hence the recency becomes a relatively important factor in the GS which can make the antecedent more accessible for the anaphor. Naturally the Continuation, the Shift, and the Link AN-pairs in the GS will be further sub-classified according to the variations [±C] of the antecedent. If the antecedent is [+C], the corresponding Continuation, Shift, and Link AN-pairs are Strong Continuation, Smooth Shift, Short Link respectively; and if the antecedent is [-C], the corresponding Continuation, Shift, and Link AN-pairs are Weak Continuation, Rough Shift, Distant Link respectively. The detail is shown below.

**Table 3.13 The Pairs of the Antecedent and the Anaphor in the GS**

| | [+T,+S] | [+T,-S] | [-T,+S] | [-T,-S] |
|---|---|---|---|---|
| [+T,+S,+C] | Strong Continuation | Strong Continuation | Smooth Shift | Smooth Shift |
| [+T,-S,+C] | Strong Continuation | Strong Continuation | Smooth Shift | Smooth Shift |
| [+T,+S,-C] | Weak Continuation | Weak Continuation | Rough Shift | Rough Shift |

| | [+T,+S] | [+T,-S] | [-T,+S] | [-T,-S] |
|---|---|---|---|---|
| [+T,-S,-C] | Weak Continuation | Weak Continuation | Rough Shift | Rough Shift |
| [-T,+S,+C] | Smooth Shift | Smooth Shift | Short Link | Short Link |
| [-T,-S,+C] | Smooth Shift | Smooth Shift | Short Link | Short Link |
| [-T,+S,-C] | Rough Shift | Rough Shift | Distant Link | Distant Link |
| [-T,-S,-C] | Rough Shift | Rough Shift | Distant Link | Distant Link |

It can be viewed from Table 3.13 that the AN-pairs in the GS include Strong / Weak Continuation, Smooth / Rough Shift, and Short / Distant Link.

#### 3.7.2.3.4 Discourse structure and the Pairs of the Antecedent and the Anaphor

As mentioned above, there are usually six kinds of AN-pairs: Strong Continuation, Weak Continuation, Smooth Shift, Rough Shift, Short Link, and Distant Link; though the detailed behaviors of the antecedent and the anaphor may vary with different kinds of super-node structures. In the MS, the tightest structural relation makes the topicality, the saliency, and referential distance all sensitive in people's cognition. In the LS, the great impact of the topicality will make the saliency and referential distance not so sensitive in people's cognition. And in the GS, there is not the structural connection as well as information relatedness, and referential distance is consequently more sensitive in people's cognition due to the recency. As a result, different super-node structures will make different variations of the antecedent and the anaphor on topicality, saliency, and referential distance become the same kind of the AN-pairs.

In a word, there are five kinds of AN-pairs in the MS: Strong Continuation, Weak Continuation, Smooth Shift, Rough Shift, and Distant Link. In the LS, there are only four kinds of AN-pairs: Strong Continuation, Weak Continuation, Short Link, and Distant Link. And in the GS, there are six kinds of AN-pairs: Strong Continuation, Weak Continuation, Smooth Shift, Rough Shift, Short Link, and Distant Link.

### 3.7.2.4 How Four Main Factors Affect the Accessibility of the Antecedent

It is argued that the impacts of four main factors on the accessibility of the antecedent are actually represented by the interaction between the impact of discourse structure and that of the pairs of the antecedent and the anaphor.

Discourse structure affects the accessibility of the antecedent through three kinds of super-node structures: the MS, the LS, and the GS. There is a ranking order of antecedents on the accessibility from different super-node structures: the Antecedents in the MS > the Antecedents in the LS > the Antecedents in the GS.

The topicality, the saliency, and referential distance affect the accessibility of the antecedent through different AN-pairs. There are totally six kinds of the pairs of the antecedent and the anaphor: Strong Continuation, Weak Continuation, Smooth Shift, Rough Shift, Short Link, and Distant Link. Different pairs of the antecedent and the anaphor can result in different degrees of accessibility of the antecedent. According to the above discussion, the complete ranking order of antecedents on the accessibility from the AN-pairs can be obtained: the Antecedents in Strong Continuation > the Antecedents in Weak Continuation > the Antecedents in Smooth Shift > the Antecedents in Rough Shift > the Antecedents in Short Link > the Antecedents in Distant Link.

As indicated above, the antecedents can be ranked by two general hierarchies on the accessibility. One is the hierarchy from super-node structures: the Antecedents in the MS > the Antecedents in the LS > the Antecedents in the GS, and the other is the hierarchy from AN-pairs: the Antecedents in Strong Continuation > the Antecedents in Weak Continuation > the Antecedents in Smooth Shift > the Antecedents in Rough Shift > the Antecedents in Short Link > the Antecedents in Distant Link.

But it is hard to combine those two hierarchies into one hierarchy. There are five, four, and six kinds of AN-pairs in the MS, the LS, and GS respectively due to the characteristics of different super-node structures. And therefore we can obtain 15 kinds of more detailed AN-pairs: Strong Continuation of the MS, Weak Continuation of the MS, Smooth Shift of the MS, Rough Shift of the MS, Distant Link of the MS, Strong Continuation of the LS, Weak Continuation of the LS, Short Link of the LS, Distant Link of the LS, Strong Continuation of the GS, Weak Continuation of the GS, Smooth Shift of the GS, Rough Shift of the GS, Short Link of the GS, and Distant Link of the GS. But it is hard to rank those 15 kinds of detailed AN-pairs on the accessibility of the antecedent, in that there is no precise significance on the super-node structures and various AN-pairs in people's cognitive status. For instance, there is no evidence to say that the accessibility of the antecedent in Smooth Shift of a MS is higher than that in Weak Continuation of a LS. Thus, it is hard to achieve a unified and precise ranking order of antecedents based on the interaction between discourse structure and the AN-pairs.

Rather than ranking all antecedents, this thesis will classify the antecedents into several distinguished sets based on super-node structures and the AN-pairs. Concretely speaking, three kinds of super-node structures will categorize all kinds of antecedents into three sets. The AN-pairs will further sub-classify those three sets of antecedents into several sub-sets, which can be illustrated by the following figure.[①]

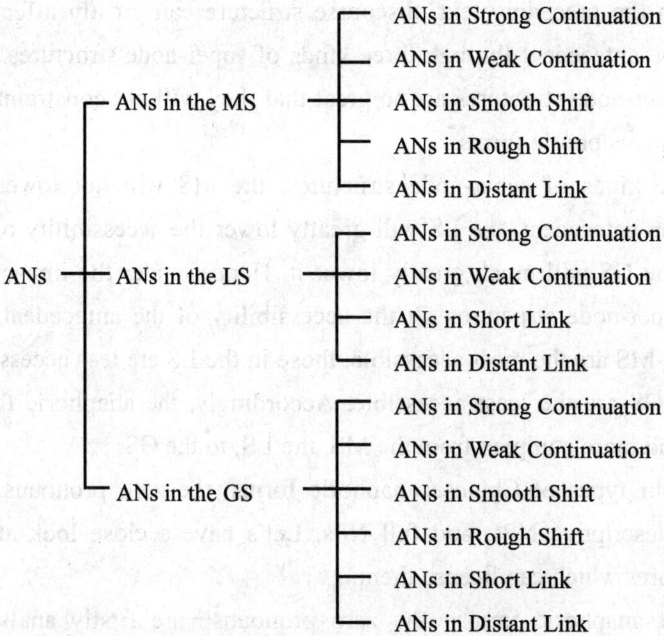


**Fig. 3.3 The Overall Ranking of Antecedents**

① "ANs" in this figure is the abbreviation of "antecedents".

As shown in Fig. 3.3, all kinds of antecedents can be categorized into some distinguished sets based on the impacts of discourse structure, topicality, saliency, and referential distance on the accessibility of the antecedent. Specifically, the super-node structures and the AN-pairs interact with each other and together impact the accessibility of the antecedent. The subsequent text will explore how their interaction affects uses of Chinese anaphoric forms.

### 3.7.3 The Interpretations on Uses of Chinese Anaphoric Forms

This part will mainly explore the explicit correlation between the accessibility of the antecedent and Chinese anaphoric forms based on the interaction between super-node structures and AN-pairs.

#### 3.7.3.1 The Constraints of Discourse Structure on Chinese Anaphoric Forms

As argued in the preceding text, discourse structure can greatly affect the accessibility of the antecedent through three kinds of super-node structures. The impacts of the super-node structures are so great that they will put constraints on the uses of Chinese anaphoric forms.

Among three kinds of super-node structures, the MS will not lower the accessibility of the antecedent, the LS will greatly lower the accessibility of the antecedent, and the GS will much greatly lower it. Hence, under the impacts of three kinds of super-node structures on the accessibility of the antecedent, the antecedents in the MS are the most accessible, those in the LS are less accessible, and those in the GS are the least accessible. Accordingly, the anaphoric forms should be more and more complex from the MS, the LS, to the GS.

There are four types of Chinese anaphoric forms: the zero pronouns, the overt pronouns, descriptive NPs, and full NPs. Let's have a close look at the super-node structures which can license them.

The simplest anaphoric forms—the zero pronouns—are firstly analyzed. Since the antecedents in the MS are the most accessible, the highest degree of accessibility of the antecedent should occur in the MS. And hence the simplest anaphoric forms—the zero pronouns—should be used to encode the highest degree of accessibility of the antecedent. Moreover, the zero pronouns only mark the highest degree of accessibility of the antecedent due to the special impact of the highest degree on people's cognitive status. The LS will greatly lower the accessibility of the antecedent, and the highest degree of accessibility of the antecedent will consequently not occur in the LS. As a result, the simplest anaphoric forms- the zero pronouns- should not occur in the LS.

Naturally, the simplest anaphoric forms of the LS become into the overt pronouns. Furthermore, the simplest anaphoric forms of the LS- the overt pronouns- will not occur in the GS due to the great lowering of the GS on the accessibility of the antecedent.

Now let's come to explore the occurring super-node structures of the most complex Chinese anaphoric forms—full NPs. The antecedents with the lowest degree of accessibility would definitely occur in a GS, and therefore the most complex Chinese anaphoric forms can occur in a GS to encode the lowest accessibility of the antecedent. The lowest degree of accessibility of the antecedent in the LS is naturally higher than that in the GS. But since each type of Chinese anaphoric forms is usually to encode a set of similar degrees rather than a special degree of accessibility of the antecedent, full NPs may occur in the LS. The MS will not permit the occurrence of full NPs, in that the lowest degree of accessibility of the antecedent in the MS is much higher than that in the GS.

Descriptive NPs are the anaphoric forms which are neither the simplest nor the most complex, and they are consequently used to mark the intermediate degrees of accessibility of the antecedent. According to the above determination of the simplest and the most complex anaphoric forms of all kinds of super-node structures, descriptive NPs can occur in the MS, the LS, as well as the GS.

Here are the detail constraints of the super-node structures on Chinese anaphoric forms.

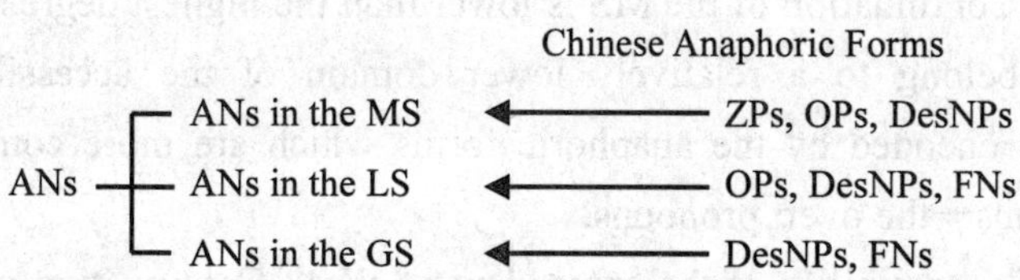


**Fig. 3.4 The Constraints of Super-node Structures on Chinese Anaphoric Forms**

This thesis will further analyze the constraints of the AN-pairs on the uses of Chinese anaphoric forms based on Fig. 3.4.

### 3.7.3.2 The Constraints of the AN-pairs on Chinese Anaphoric Forms

The AN-pairs will further constraint uses of Chinese anaphoric forms based on the constraints of the super-node structures.

Let's begin to analyze the constraints of the AN-pairs from the highest degree of accessibility of the antecedent. When the antecedent occurs in Strong Continuation as well as a MS, its degree of accessibility is the highest, and should consequently be marked by the simplest anaphoric form—the zero pronouns. The accessibility of the antecedent which occurs in the Strong Continuation of the LS is much lower than that of the antecedent which occurs in the Strong Continuation of the MS, in that the LS will greatly lower the accessibility of the antecedent. And therefore the antecedent of Strong Continuation of the LS should be referred back by the anaphoric forms which are more complex than the zero pronouns—the overt pronouns. For the same reason, the antecedents of Strong Continuation of the GS should be referred back by a type of Chinese anaphoric forms which are more complex than the overt pronouns—descriptive NPs. Thus, the correlation between Strong Continuation of the AN-pairs and Chinese anaphoric forms can be obtained, which is illustrated below.[①]

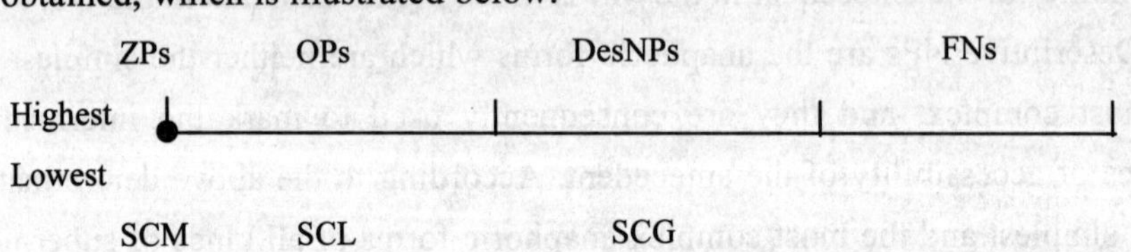


**Fig. 3.5 The Correlation between Strong Continuation and Chinese Anaphoric forms**

In respect of Weak Continuation, the degree of accessibility of the antecedent of Weak Continuation of the MS is lower than the highest degree, and they consequently belong to a relatively lower domain of the accessibility continuum which is encoded by the anaphoric forms which are more complex than the zero pronouns—the overt pronouns.

The degrees of accessibility of the antecedent of Weak Continuation of the

① SCM, SCL, and SCG are to express Strong Continuation in the MS, the LS, and the GS respectively.

LS are lower than that of Strong Continuation of the LS, and should not be encoded by the same type of anaphoric forms. But they also cannot be encoded only by the more complex type of Chinese anaphoric forms—descriptive NPs, because the typical degrees of accessibility encoded by descriptive NPs are those resulted from Strong Continuation of the GS. Since the impact of the saliency and referential distance on the accessibility of the antecedent will not be as great as that of the GS, Weak Continuation of the LS and Strong Continuation of the GS will not result in similar degrees of accessibility of the antecedent. Rather than that, the degrees of accessibility of the antecedent resulted from Weak Continuation of the LS are higher than those resulted from Strong Continuation of the GS. Hence the degrees of accessibility of the antecedent of Weak Continuation of the LS should be in the middle of two domains which are encoded by the overt pronouns and descriptive NPs respectively. Thus, the antecedents of Weak Continuation of LS will not result in the typical uses of any type of Chinese anaphoric forms, but can be referred back either by the overt pronouns or by descriptive NPs. For the same reason, the antecedents of Weak Continuation of the GS could be referred by descriptive NPs as well as full NPs.

The following is the correlation between Weak Continuation and the uses of Chinese anaphoric forms.①

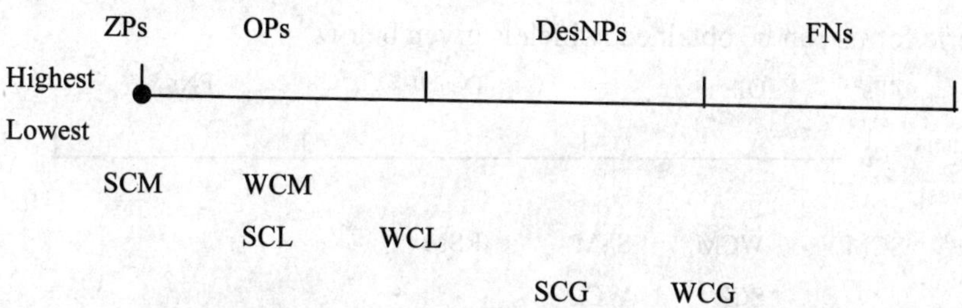


**Fig. 3.6 The Correlation between weak Continuation and Chinese Anaphoric forms**

As to the Shift pairs of the antecedent and the anaphor, there are two kinds of detailed AN-pairs: Smooth Shift and Rough Shift. The LS has no Shift AN-pair. Therefore we only consider Smooth Shift and Rough Shift in the MS and the GS.

The degree of accessibility of the antecedent of Smooth Shift of the MS is

① WCM, WCL, and WCG are to express Weak Continuation in the MS, the LS, and the GS respectively.

lower than those of Weak Continuation of the MS. Since the change of the accessibility of the antecedent is gradual, the degree of accessibility of the antecedent of Smooth Shift of the MS should be in the middle of two domains which are encoded by the overt pronouns and descriptive NPs respectively. The degree of accessibility of the antecedent of Rough Shift of the MS is further lower than those of Smooth Shift of the MS, and thus belongs to the domain which is encoded by descriptive NPs.

The degree of accessibility of the antecedent of Smooth Shift of the GS is lower than those of Weak Continuation of the GS. Since the degree of accessibility of the antecedent of Weak Continuation of the GS is in the middle of two domains which are encoded by descriptive NPs and full NPs respectively, the degree of accessibility of the antecedent of Smooth Shift of the GS should belong to the domain which is encoded by full NPs. The degree of accessibility of the antecedent of Rough Shift of the GS is further lower than those of Smooth Shift of the GS. But as the degrees of accessibility of the antecedent of Smooth Shift of the GS are encoded by the most complex anaphoric forms—full NPs, other lower degrees should be also encoded by full NPs. As a consequence, the antecedents of either Smooth Shift or Rough Shift of the GS should be referred back by full NPs.

Hence the correlation between the Shift AN-pairs and the uses of Chinese anaphoric forms can be obtained, which is given below.①

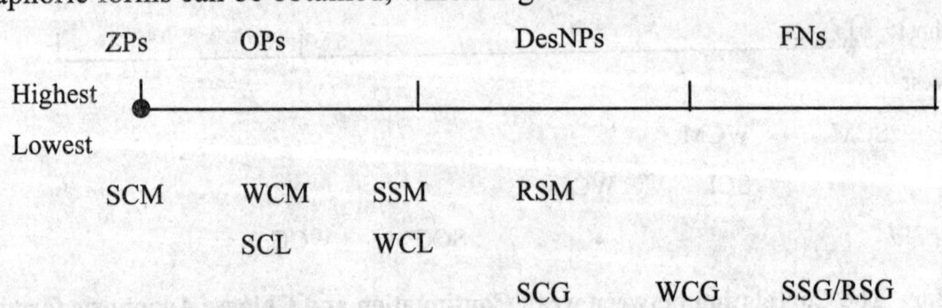


**Fig. 3.7　The Correlation between the Shift and Chinese Anaphoric forms**

As far as the Link is concerned, the degree of accessibility of the antecedent of Short Link of the LS is lower than those of Weak Continuation of the LS, and

① SSM, RSM, SSG, and RSG are to express Smooth Shift in the MS, Rough Shift in the MS, Smooth Shift in the GS, and Rough Shift in the GS respectively.

should be encoded by a distinctive type of anaphoric forms which are descriptive NPs. The degree of accessibility of the antecedent of Distant Link of the LS is further lower than those of Short Link of the LS, and then it would go to the middle between two domains due to the gradual characteristics of the accessibility continuum which are encoded by descriptive NPs and full NPs respectively. As a result, the antecedents of Short Link of the LS should be referred back by descriptive NPs and those of Distant Link of the LS could be referred back by either descriptive NPs or full NPs.

As to the degree of accessibility of the antecedent of Distant Link of the MS, they are higher than those of Distant Link of the LS. Since the degrees of accessibility of the antecedent of Distant Link of the LS are encoded by either descriptive NPs or full NPs, those of Distant Link of the MS should be encoded only by descriptive NPs.

The degree of accessibility of the antecedent of Short Link as well as Distant Link of the GS is lower than those of the Shift of the GS. As the degrees of accessibility of the antecedent of the Shift of the GS all are encoded by the most complex anaphoric forms—full NPs, those of the Link, Short Link as well as Distant Link, of the GS should be also encoded by full NPs.

Here is the correlation between the AN-pairs and Chinese anaphoric forms.①

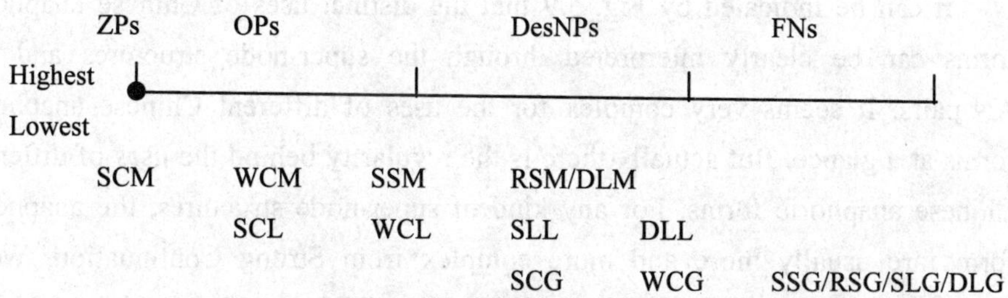


**Fig. 3.8 The correlation between the AN-pairs and chinese anaphoric forms**

According to the discussions in the preceding texts, three kinds of super-node structures categorize all kinds of antecedents into three sets, and the

① DLM, SLL, DLL, SLG, and DLG are to express Distant Link in the MS, Short Link in the LS, Distant Link in the LS, Short Link in the GS, and Distant Link in the GS respectively.

AN-pairs further classify those three sets of antecedents into more detailed subsets. Hence the correlation between each subset of antecedents and the uses of Chinese anaphoric forms can be given below.

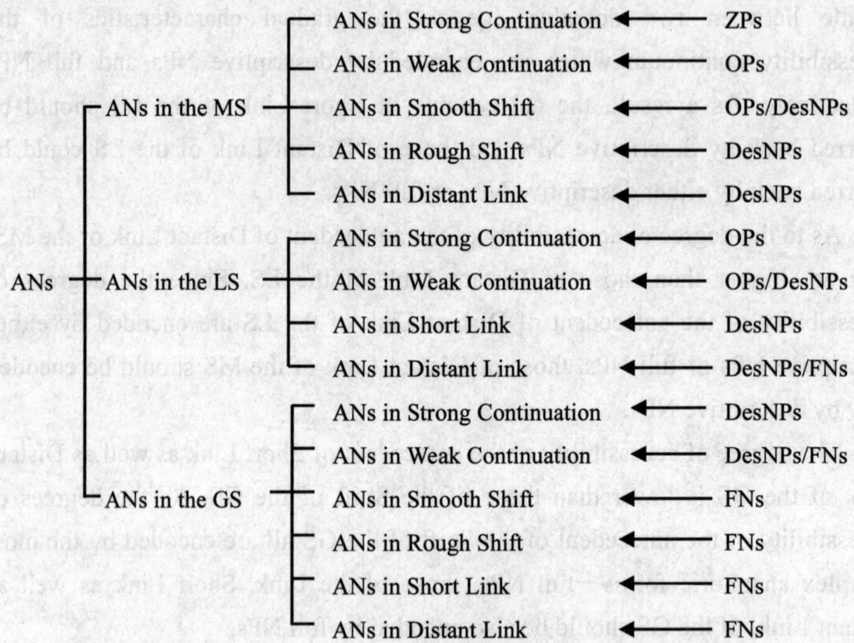


**Fig. 3.9 The Correlation between antecedents and Chinese anaphoric forms**

It can be indicated by Fig. 3.9 that the distinct uses of Chinese anaphoric forms can be clearly interpreted through the super-node structures and the AN-pairs. It seems very complex for the uses of different Chinese anaphoric forms at a glance. But actually there is the regularity behind the uses of different Chinese anaphoric forms. For any kind of super-node structures, the anaphoric forms are usually more and more complex from Strong Continuation, Weak Continuation, Smooth Shift, Rough Shift, Short Link, to Distant Link. And For any kind of the AN-pairs, the anaphoric forms are usually more and more complex from the MS, the LS, to the GS.

It is also revealed from Fig. 3.9 that the super-node structures and the AN-pairs are indispensable and complementary in the interpretations on the uses of Chinese anaphoric forms. Discourse structure and the AN-pairs are indivisible for the interpretations on the uses of Chinese anaphoric forms. Discourse structure will make the AN-pairs more various on the accessibility of the antecedent, and the AN-pairs will make discourse structure more concrete on the accessibility of the antecedent. To combine discourse structure and the AN-pairs can obtain the complete accessibility of the antecedent and further find out the correlation between the accessibility of the antecedent and Chinese anaphoric forms.

Generally speaking, all kinds of antecedents can be categorized into a number of groups. Different groups of antecedents will result in the distinguished impacts on people's cognitive status due to the effect of discourse structure, topicality, saliency, and referential distance on the accessibility of the antecedent, and are consequently correlated closely with the uses of Chinese anaphoric forms. After the detailed analysis on the impact of those four main factors on the accessibility of the antecedent, the explicit relationship between Chinese anaphoric forms and different groups of antecedents can be achieved.

#### 3.7.3.3 The Accessibility Marking Hierarchy of Chinese Anaphoric Forms

So far, this thesis has analyzed the impact of discourse structure, topicality, saliency, and referential distance on the accessibility of the antecedent in detail, and further differentiated four distinct domains of the accessibility continuum of the antecedent, and finally correlated those four distinct domains with four types of Chinese anaphoric forms.

According to the above discussions, the distinct uses of Chinese anaphoric forms are actually accordant to the general statements of anaphoric forms in the previous research. There is a reverse relation between the descriptive information of anaphoric forms and the degree of accessibility of the antecedent. The simpler anaphoric forms are to mark higher accessibility of the antecedent, and the more complex anaphoric forms are to mark lower accessibility of the antecedent. Thus, the Accessibility Marking Hierarchy of Chinese anaphoric forms can be established: zero pronouns > overt pronouns (the third-person pronoun / the definite pronouns) > descriptive NPs > full NPs.

It should be noted that the above Accessibility Marking Hierarchy of Chinese anaphoric forms is a general marking hierarchy of all kinds of Chinese anaphoric forms. The general Accessibility Marking Hierarchy has different performances in different contexts. The different performances are mainly reflected with distinct super-node structures. As discourse structure is proposed to greatly affect the accessibility of the antecedent, it can put constraints on their permitted anaphoric expressions. And the general Accessibility Marking Hierarchy will consequently have different behaviors in distinct super-node structures. For instance, full NPs are blocked in the MS, then the Accessibility Marking Hierarchy of Chinese anaphoric forms in the MS will not include full NPs, which is represented as: zero pronouns > overt pronouns (the third-person pronoun / the definite pronouns) > descriptive NPs. In the same way, there is a special hierarchy of the accessibility deviation in the LS as well as the GS. The Accessibility Marking Hierarchy in the LS is: overt pronouns (the third-person pronoun / the definite pronouns) > descriptive NPs > full NPs, and that in the GS is: descriptive NPs > full NPs. More left are the anaphoric forms, higher degrees of accessibility of the antecedent they are to encode.

Generally speaking, discourse structure can affect the behaviors of the general Accessibility Marking Hierarchy in different super-node structures and make the occurrence of all kinds of Chinese anaphoric forms more complicated. There are different kinds of Chinese anaphoric forms in different super-node structures, on the one hand; some kind of Chinese anaphoric forms can occur in more than one kind of super-node structures, on the other hand. So we have to figure out the impact of discourse structure on the uses of Chinese anaphoric forms. Otherwise, different uses of various kinds of Chinese anaphoric forms can not be clearly revealed, and the correlation between different Chinese anaphoric forms cannot be rightly found, and therefore the Accessibility Marking Hierarchy of Chinese anaphoric forms cannot be obtained. In short, discourse structure plays an important role in the interpretations of Chinese anaphoric forms. And the general Accessibility Marking Hierarchy of Chinese anaphoric forms will have some variations due to the impact of discourse structure on the interpretations of Chinese anaphoric forms.

But no matter how the Accessibility Marking Hierarchy varies in different super-node structures, the uses of all kinds of Chinese anaphoric forms always keep to the general Accessibility Marking Hierarchy. For instance, *ta* can occur in the MS as well as in the LS, but it is always to mark the degrees of accessibility of antecedents which are lower than the highest degree of accessibility.

The above is the whole process of the interpretations on the uses of Chinese anaphoric forms from the conceptual view. Briefly speaking, this thesis has suggested the main factors which can affect the accessibility of the antecedent and further analyzed them from a new perspective, and finally can well interpret the distinct uses of Chinese anaphoric forms.

## 3.8 Summary

This chapter has interpreted distinct uses of various Chinese anaphoric forms with a set of theoretical notions.

We have firstly tried to identify the main factors affecting uses of Chinese anaphoric forms. The claim that different anaphors are linguistic markers for the accessibility degree of the antecedent is crucial for the interpretations of Chinese anaphoric forms of this thesis. Furthermore, discourse structure, topicality, saliency and referential distance are proposed as four main factors which affect the uses of Chinese anaphoric forms since they can affect the accessibility of the antecedent.

Secondly, how discourse structure, topicality, saliency and referential distance affect uses of Chinese anaphoric forms have been analyzed. Discourse structure affects the accessibility of the antecedent through three kinds of super-node structures: the MS, the LS, and the GS. Topicality, saliency, and referential distance affect the accessibility of the antecedent through the AN-pairs. Six kinds of the AN-pairs are proposed: Strong Continuation, Weak Continuation, Smooth Shift, Rough Shift, Short Link, and Distant Link.

Thirdly, this thesis further analyzes the interaction between discourse structure and the pairs of the antecedent and the anaphor on the accessibility of the antecedent and obtains four distinct domains of the accessibility continuum of the antecedent.

Finally, based on the distinct domains of the accessibility continuum of the antecedent, the clear relationship between Chinese anaphoric forms and degrees of accessibility of the antecedent can be obtained, and moreover the distinct uses of various Chinese anaphoric forms can be clearly revealed from the conceptual analysis. Besides that, a general Accessibility Marking Hierarchy of Chinese anaphoric forms is proposed and the special behaviors of the Accessibility Marking Hierarchy are discussed.

# Chapter 4 A Corpus-based Study on Chinese Anaphoric Forms

In this chapter, I will begin by investigating the distributions of Chinese anaphoric forms in written discourse of Mandarin, and then compare the behaviors of various anaphoric forms in the corpus and the theoretical interpretations proposed in chapter 3. I will eventually illustrate the validity of the interpretations of Chinese anaphoric forms of this thesis based on the corpus-based study.

## 4.1 The Corpus

The corpus-based study in this thesis investigates the distributions of Chinese anaphoric forms in the Chinese corpus of City University of Hong Kong. The corpus consists of 115 written articles of 220,972 Chinese characters in Mandarin. But this thesis will not include all articles of the corpus. Only 51 randomly selected articles including 111,210 Chinese characters of six kinds of genres are selected as data for investigation. Those six kinds of genres are described here: *Narratives*, *Proses*, *Expositions*, *Arguments, Poems,* and *Reports.* The components of the corpus are illustrated below.

Table 4.1　Components of the Corpus

| | Number of Articles | Percentage of Articles | Number of Characters | Percentage of Characters |
|---|---|---|---|---|
| Narratives | 25 | 49.02% | 57,193 | 51.43% |
| Proses | 12 | 23.53% | 20,425 | 18.37% |
| Expositions | 7 | 13.73% | 19,172 | 17.24% |
| Arguments | 2 | 3.92% | 6,907 | 6.21% |
| Poems | 2 | 3.92% | 1,381 | 1.24% |
| Reports | 3 | 5.88% | 6,132 | 5.51% |
| Total | 51 | 100% | 111,210 | 100% |

As Table 4.1 indicates, *Narratives* account for the largest part of the corpus with 51.43% of the total data. *Proses* come next with 18.37%, and *Poems* are the smallest component accounting for only 1.24% of the corpus.

## 4.2 Distributions of Chinese Anaphoric Forms in the Corpus

Chapter 3 has studied the interpretations of Chinese anaphoric forms in detail. Briefly speaking, the distinctive behaviors of Chinese anaphoric forms can be well interpreted by the interaction between the super-node structures based on the discourse structure and the AN-pairs based on the topicality, the salience, and referential distance with their impacts on the accessibility of the antecedent.

Hence three aspects should be taken into account in the corpus-based study: 1) distributions of Chinese anaphoric forms on distinct super-node structures; 2) distributions of the AN-pairs, and 3) distributions of Chinese anaphoric forms based on the interaction between super-node structures and the AN-pairs. After examining the above three issues, detailed uses of Chinese anaphoric forms in the corpus can be clearly revealed and can then be compared with the conceptual interpretations on uses of Chinese anaphoric forms as discussed in chapter 3.

### 4.2.1 Distributions of Zero Pronouns

Zero pronouns are often used in the corpus. Its detailed distribution in different super-node structures is shown below.

**Table 4.2 The Distribution of Zero Pronouns In SUPER-NODE STRUCTURES**

| | Zero Pronoun in MS | Zero Pronoun in LS | Zero Pronoun in GS | Total |
|---|---|---|---|---|
| Numbers of ZPs | 2001 | 21 | 0 | 2022 |
| Percentage of ZPs | 98.96% | 1.04% | 0% | 100% |

According to Table 4.2, most of zero pronouns occur in the MS. There are 2001 zero pronouns in the MS, which reaches 98.96%. Only a few zero pronouns occur in the LS, which just take up 1.04%. And there is no zero pronouns in the GS.

The interaction between super-node structures and the AN-pairs on the zero pronouns is illustrated by the following table.

**Table 4.3 The Distribution of the Zero Pronoun In the Super-node Structures and the Pairs of the Antecedent and the Anaphor**

| Super-node Structures | The AN-pairs | Numbers of ZP | Percentage of ZP |
|---|---|---|---|
| MS | Strong Continuation | 1965 | 97.18% |
| | Weak Continuation | 4 | 0.20% |
| | Smooth Shift | 32 | 1.58% |
| | Rough Shift | 0 | 0% |
| | Distant Link | 0 | 0% |
| LS | Strong Continuation | 21 | 1.04% |
| | Weak Continuation | 0 | 0% |
| | Short Link | 0 | 0% |
| | Distant Link | 0 | 0% |
| GS | Strong Continuation | 0 | 0% |
| | Weak Continuation | 0 | 0% |
| | Smooth Shift | 0 | 0% |
| | Rough Shift | 0 | 0% |
| | Short Link | 0 | 0% |
| | Distant Link | 0 | 0% |
| Total | | 2022 | 100% |

It is obvious from Table 4.3 that, the uses of zero pronouns are very concentrated: 97.18% of zero pronouns are used in Strong Continuation of the MS, while only a small part of the zero pronouns will occur in the other AN-pairs. Hence there is a strong tendency of the distribution of the zero pronoun in the super-node structures and the AN-pairs.

According to the conceptual interpretations of Chinese anaphoric forms discussed in chapter 3, the zero pronoun is the simplest anaphoric form in Chinese, and therefore it is proposed to encode the highest degree of accessibility of the antecedent which is actually resulted from Strong Continuation of a MS. So the actual uses of almost all zero pronouns in the corpus are accordant with the conceptual interpretations of Chinese anaphoric forms in chapter 3, though few zero pronouns violate the conceptual interpretations.

### 4.2.2 Distributions of Overt Pronouns

Two kinds of pronouns are found in Chinese overt pronouns: the third-person pronoun *ta* and the proximal/distal pronoun *zhe/na*. Those two kinds of overt pronouns are almost the same in terms of referring to a descriptive content, and they should consequently mark the same domain of the accessibility continuum of the antecedent. Firstly, let's have a close look at the distribution of different overt pronouns in distinct super-node structures, which are shown in Table 4.4.

**Table 4.4　The Distributions of Overt Pronouns in Super-node structures**

| | Overt Pronouns in MS | Overt Pronouns in LS | Overt Pronouns in GS | Total |
|---|---|---|---|---|
| Numbers of *ta* | 308 | 330 | 17 | 655 |
| Percentage of *ta* | 47.02% | 50.38% | 2.60% | 100% |
| Numbers of *zhe/na* | 8 | 8 | 0 | 16 |
| Percentage of *zhe/na* | 50% | 50% | 0% | 100% |
| Numbers of OPs | 316 | 338 | 17 | 671 |
| Percentage of OPs | 47.10% | 50.37% | 2.53% | 100% |

It is obvious in Table 4.4 that the numbers of the third-person pronoun *ta* is greater than those of the proximal/distal pronouns *zhe/na*s: there are 655 instances of *ta* in the corpus, while there are only 16 *zhe/nas*. The unbalanced distributions between the two kinds of overt pronouns are resulted from some restriction of the proximal/distal pronouns on the space. But that kind of unbalanced distributions will not challenge of the interpretations of Chinese anaphoric forms in this thesis.

In addition, it can be seen from Table 4.4 that the distribution of Chinese overt pronouns in super-node structures is much different from that of the zero pronoun. Almost all of zero pronouns concentrate only in the MS, few of them occurs in the LS, and none of them occurs in the GS; while 316 (47.10%) and 338 (50.37%) overt pronouns occur in MS and the LS respectively, and only 17 (2.60%) overt pronouns occur in the GS. Hence the uses of Chinese overt pronoun are not as concentrated as those of zero pronouns in the corpus from the super-node structures.

Now let's have a further look at Chinese anaphora with overt pronouns. The detailed patterns of Chinese anaphora with overt pronouns need to be further explored. Since there are two kinds of overt pronouns, this thesis will investigate the distributions of those two kinds of overt pronouns separately so that the explicit uses of overt pronouns can be figured out.

Below is the detailed distribution of *ta*s in the super-node structures and the AN-pairs.

**Table 4.5 The Distribution of tas In the Super-node Structures and the Pairs of the Antecedent and the Anaphor**

| Super-node Structures | The AN-pairs | Numbers of *tas* | Percentage of *tas* |
|---|---|---|---|
| MS | Strong Continuation | 7 | 1.07% |
| | Weak Continuation | 219 | 33.43% |
| | Smooth Shift | 64 | 9.77% |
| | Rough Shift | 18 | 2.75% |
| | Distant Link | 0 | 0% |
| LS | Strong Continuation | 272 | 41.53% |
| | Weak Continuation | 55 | 8.40% |
| | Short Link | 0 | 0% |
| | Distant Link | 3 | 0.46% |

| Super-node Structures | The AN-pairs | Numbers of *tas* | Percentage of *tas* |
|---|---|---|---|
| GS | Strong Continuation | 9 | 1.37% |
| | Weak Continuation | 8 | 1.22% |
| | Smooth Shift | 0 | 0% |
| | Rough Shift | 0 | 0% |
| | Short Link | 0 | 0% |
| | Distant Link | 0 | 0% |
| Total | | 655 | 100% |

It can be found from Table 4.5 that *ta is* most commonly used in Strong Continuation of the LS, which arrives at 41.53%. And *ta*s secondly occur in Weak Continuation of the MS, which takes up 33.43%. Only a small part of *ta*s is used in Smooth Shift of the MS and Weak Continuation of the LS, which take 9.77% and 8.40% respectively. And *ta*s seldom occur in other kinds of the AN-pairs.

The uses of the proximal/distal pronouns *zhe*/*na* are much simpler than that of *ta*. Here is the detail distribution of *zhe*/*na*s in the super-node structures and the AN-pairs.

**Table 4.6　The Distribution of zhe/nas In the Super-node Structures and the Pairs of the Antecedent and the Anaphor**

| Super-node Structures | The AN-pairs | Numbers of *zhe*/*na*s | Percentage of *zhe*/*na*s |
|---|---|---|---|
| MS | Strong Continuation | 0 | 0% |
| | Weak Continuation | 0 | 0% |
| | Smooth Shift | 8 | 50% |
| | Rough Shift | 0 | 0% |
| | Distant Link | 0 | 0% |
| LS | Strong Continuation | 8 | 50% |
| | Weak Continuation | 0 | 0% |
| | Short Link | 0 | 0% |
| | Distant Link | 0 | 0% |

| Super-node Structures | The AN-pairs | Numbers of *zhe/na*s | Percentage of *zhe/nas* |
|---|---|---|---|
| GS | Strong Continuation | 0 | 0% |
| | Weak Continuation | 0 | 0% |
| | Smooth Shift | 0 | 0% |
| | Rough Shift | 0 | 0% |
| | Short Link | 0 | 0% |
| | Distant Link | 0 | 0% |
| Total | | 16 | 100% |

The general distributions of Chinese overt pronouns on the super-node structures and the AN-pairs are given below.

**Table 4.7 The Distribution of Chinese Overt Pronouns on the Super-node Structures and the Pairs of the Antecedent and the Anaphor**

| Super-node Structures | The AN-pairs | Numbers of OPs | Percentage of OPs |
|---|---|---|---|
| MS | Strong Continuation | 7 | 1.04% |
| | Weak Continuation | 219 | 32.64% |
| | Smooth Shift | 72 | 10.73% |
| | Rough Shift | 18 | 2.68% |
| | Distant Link | 0 | 0% |
| LS | Strong Continuation | 280 | 41.73% |
| | Weak Continuation | 55 | 8.20% |
| | Short Link | 0 | 0% |
| | Distant Link | 3 | 0.45% |
| GS | Strong Continuation | 9 | 1.34% |
| | Weak Continuation | 8 | 1.19% |
| | Smooth Shift | 0 | 0% |
| | Rough Shift | 0 | 0% |
| | Short Link | 0 | 0% |
| | Distant Link | 0 | 0% |
| Total | | 671 | 100% |

It can be found from Table 4.7 that there is a strong regularity in the corpus uses of Chinese overt pronouns which are mainly used in Weak Continuation of the MS and Strong Continuation of the LS and partly used in Smooth Shift of the MS and Weak Continuation of the LS.

It is proposed in the interpretations of Chinese anaphoric forms as discussed in chapter 3 that Chinese overt pronouns are to encode the lightly deviated degrees from the highest accessibility of the antecedent. Briefly, the overt pronouns should be chiefly used to encode the degrees of accessibility of the antecedent in Weak Continuation of the MS and Strong Continuation of the LS. The anaphor can also be encoded by the overt pronouns in Smooth Shift of the MS or in Weak Continuation of the LS due to the fuzzy property between different continuous degrees of accessibility; in which different deviated degrees will be reflected by the proportions of Chinese overt pronouns on different AN-pairs with different super-node structures.

The corpus data of Chinese anaphora with overt pronouns provide strong evidence to support the conceptual interpretations on Chinese overt pronouns. The total proportion of Chinese overt pronouns in Weak Continuation of the MS and Strong Continuation of the LS are 74.37%, which are the major usage patterns of Chinese overt pronouns according to the conceptual interpretations of Chinese anaphoric forms; while the proportions of Chinese overt pronouns in Smooth Shift of the MS and in Weak Continuation of the LS are 18.93%, which is the possible uses of overt pronouns according to the conceptual interpretations on overt pronouns. There are only 6.7% of Chinese overt pronouns in the corpus which violate the conceptual interpretations on Chinese overt pronouns.

Thus, it can be concluded from the above corpus data that the uses of Chinese overt pronouns are basically accordant with the interpretations of Chinese anaphoric forms in chapter 3.

### 4.2.3 Distributions of Descriptive NPs

Descriptive NPs mainly include two kinds of NPs: *zhe*+NPs and *na*+NPs. The distribution of descriptive NPs in distinct super-node structures is given below.

**Table 4.8 The Distribution of Descriptive NPs in Super-node structures**

| | DesNPs in MS | DesNPs in LS | DesNPs in GS | Total |
|---|---|---|---|---|
| Numbers of *zhe*+NPs | 33 | 90 | 17 | 140 |
| Percentage of *zhe*+NPs | 23.57% | 64.29% | 12.14% | 100% |
| Numbers of *na*+NPs | 10 | 36 | 17 | 63 |
| Percentage of *na*+NPs | 15.87% | 57.14% | 26.99% | 100% |
| Numbers of DesNPs | 43 | 126 | 34 | 203 |
| Percentage of DesNPs | 21.18% | 62.07% | 16.75% | 100% |

According to Table 4.8, the occurrence of super-node structures of descriptive NPs is more widely than those of the overt pronouns: descriptive NPs can occur in all kinds of super-node structures with different proportions. Descriptive NPs most often occur in the LS, which takes up 62.07%. They secondly often occur in the MS, which takes up 21.18%. And they least often occur in the GS, which only has 16.75%.

The interaction between the super-node structures and the AN-pairs is shown below.

**Table 4.9 The Distribution of Descriptive NPs In the Super-node Structures and the Pairs of the Antecedent and the Anaphor**

| Super-node Structures | The AN-pairs | Numbers of DesNPs | Percentage of DesNPs |
|---|---|---|---|
| MS | Strong Continuation | 0 | 0% |
| | Weak Continuation | 0 | 0% |
| | Smooth Shift | 11 | 5.42% |
| | Rough Shift | 2 | 0.98% |
| | Distant Link | 30 | 14.78% |
| LS | Strong Continuation | 13 | 6.40% |
| | Weak Continuation | 19 | 9.36% |
| | Short Link | 60 | 29.55% |
| | Distant Link | 34 | 16.75% |

| Super-node Structures | The AN-pairs | Numbers of DesNPs | Percentage of DesNPs |
|---|---|---|---|
| GS | Strong Continuation | 10 | 4.93% |
| | Weak Continuation | 7 | 3.45% |
| | Smooth Shift | 6 | 2.96% |
| | Rough Shift | 10 | 4.93% |
| | Short Link | 1 | 0.49% |
| | Distant Link | 0 | 0% |
| Total | | 203 | 100% |

As Table 4.9 indicates, the uses of descriptive NPs in Chinese corpus are more various than those of other kinds of Chinese anaphoric forms in the super-node structures as well as in the AN-pairs. In the MS, descriptive NPs are mainly used in Distant Link (14.78%); in the LS, they are chiefly used in Short Link (29.55%); and in the GS, they are mostly used in the Continuation types (8.38%). It seems that the uses of descriptive NPs are so complicated that it is difficult to tell the nature of them. But the above various kinds of distributions of descriptive NPs can be explained by the interpretations of Chinese anaphoric forms outlined in chapter 3.

It is argued in the conceptual interpretations of Chinese anaphoric forms that Chinese descriptive NPs are to encode the heavily deviated degrees from the highest accessibility of the antecedent. Descriptive NPs are proposed to be mainly used in Distant Link of the MS, Short Link of the LS, and the Continuation types of the GS which are just the main uses of descriptive NPs in different super-node structures in the corpus. Moreover, the neighbor AN-pairs in different super-node structures can also use descriptive NPs as a kind of untypical means to encode the degree of accessibility of the antecedent due to the fuzzy property of the accessibility continuum.

To sum up, in the corpus, 85.22% of the descriptive NPs follow the conceptual interpretations of the descriptive NPs as reported in chapter 3. Though there are some uses of descriptive NPs in the corpus which violate the interpretations of Chinese anaphoric forms, the proportion of over 80% can fully support the conceptual prediction of chapter 3. Hence it can be concluded that the corpus data of different uses of descriptive NPs is agreeable with the interpretations on the uses of Chinese anaphoric forms in chapter 3.

### 4.2.4 Distributions of Full NPs

Full NPs are regarded as one kind of Chinese anaphoric forms in this thesis. The distribution of Full NPs in super-node structures is given by Table 4.10.

**Table 4.10 The Distribution of Full NPs in super-node structures**

| | Full NPs in MS | Full NPs in LS | Full NPs in GS | Total |
|---|---|---|---|---|
| Numbers of Full NPs | 2 | 287 | 495 | 784 |
| Percentage of Full NPs | 0.25% | 36.61% | 63.14% | 100% |

According to Table 4.10, the proportions of Full NPs in the MS, the LS, and the GS are 0.25%, 36.61%, and 63.14% respectively; which shows the trend of gradual increase from the MS to the LS to the GS.

Here is the detailed distribution of full NPs in the super-node structures and the AN-pairs.

**Table 4.11 The Distribution of Full NPs In the Super-node Structures and the Pairs of the Antecedent and the Anaphor**

| Super-node Structures | The AN-pairs | Numbers of FNs | Percentage of FNs |
|---|---|---|---|
| MS | Strong Continuation | 0 | 0% |
| | Weak Continuation | 2 | 0.26% |
| | Smooth Shift | 0 | 0% |
| | Rough Shift | 0 | 0% |
| | Distant Link | 0 | 0% |
| LS | Strong Continuation | 25 | 3.19% |
| | Weak Continuation | 14 | 1.79% |
| | Short Link | 55 | 7.01% |
| | Distant Link | 193 | 24.62% |

| Super-node Structures | The AN-pairs | Numbers of FNs | Percentage of FNs |
|---|---|---|---|
| GS | Strong Continuation | 11 | 1.40% |
| | Weak Continuation | 76 | 9.69% |
| | Smooth Shift | 57 | 7.27% |
| | Rough Shift | 195 | 24.87% |
| | Short Link | 9 | 1.15% |
| | Distant Link | 147 | 18.75% |
| Total | | 784 | 100% |

According to Table 4.11, the uses of Full NPs in the corpus concentrate on Distant Link of the LS, Rough Shift of the GS, and Distant Link of the GS, which take up 24.62%, 24.87%, and 18.75% respectively. And moreover, a majority of full NPs are used in the GS, which is accordant with the constraints of the super-node structures on the uses of Chinese anaphoric forms.

In fact the corpus data of Full NPs can be well accounted for by the interpretations of Chinese anaphoric forms in chapter 3.

Since Full NPs include so many descriptive contents themselves, they are required to mark the very low even the lowest degrees of accessibility of the antecedent in the interpretations. That can firstly explain the distributions of full NPs in the super-node structures, in which full NPs occasionally occur in the MS but mostly occur in the LS or the GS. As the MS will not make the accessibility of the antecedent very low due to the impact of the MS, no matter how the AN-pairs vary, there is no need to use full NPs as the anaphoric form. But the very low or the lowest degree of accessibility of the antecedent can be observed in the LS and GS, and full NPs can consequently become the anaphoric form in the LS and the GS.

Furthermore, full NPs concentrate on the AN-pairs of the LS and the GS which can render very low or the lowest degrees of accessibility of the antecedent. According to the analysis in chapter 3, the accessibility of the antecedent which is resulted from Distant Link of the LS and five kinds of the AN-pairs of the GS except of Strong Continuation all can be marked by full NPs. There are 86.35% of

Full NPs in the corpus which are used to mark the accessibility of the antecedent which is resulted from those six kinds of the AN-pairs. I believe, 86.35% of Full NPs in the corpus can support the conceptual interpretations of Chinese anaphoric forms in chapter 3.

## 4.3 A Comparison between the Corpus Distributions and the Conceptual Interpretations of Chinese Anaphoric Forms

The previous section has investigated the detailed distributions of all kinds of Chinese anaphoric forms in the corpus. The majority of the uses of Chinese anaphoric forms in the corpus follow the conceptual interpretations of Chinese anaphoric forms as discussed in chapter 3. This section, on the other hand, will put the distributions of all Chinese anaphoric forms together and further compare the corpus distributions of various Chinese anaphoric forms with the conceptual interpretations in detail.

### 4.3.1 Distributions of Anaphoric Forms in Diverse Discourse Structures

The four distinct kinds of anaphoric forms in Chinese anaphors system: the zero pronoun, overt pronouns including the third-person pronoun *ta* and the proximal/distal pronoun *zhe/na*, descriptive NPs, and Full NPs, have the following distributions in the super-node structures, as shown in Table 4.12.

**Table 4.12 The Distributions of Chinese Anaphoric form In super-node structures**

| | Anaphors in MS | Anaphors in LS | Anaphors in GS | Total |
|---|---|---|---|---|
| Numbers of Zero Pronouns | 2001 | 21 | 0 | 2022 |
| Percentage of Zero Pronouns | 98.96% | 1.04% | 0% | 100% |
| Numbers of Overt Pronouns | 316 | 338 | 17 | 671 |
| Percentage of Overt Pronouns | 47.10% | 50.37% | 2.53% | 100% |

| | Anaphors in MS | Anaphors in LS | Anaphors in GS | Total |
|---|---|---|---|---|
| Numbers of DesNPs | 43 | 126 | 34 | 203 |
| Percentage of DesNPs | 21.18% | 62.07% | 16.75% | 100% |
| Numbers of Full NPs | 2 | 287 | 495 | 784 |
| Percentage of Full NPs | 0.25% | 36.61% | 63.14% | 100% |
| Numbers of Anaphoric Forms | 2362 | 772 | 546 | 3680 |
| Percentage of Anaphoric Forms | 64.18% | 20.98% | 14.84% | 100% |

It can be viewed from Table 4.12 that there is a very strong trend of the occurrence of different kinds of Chinese anaphoric forms in different super-node structures.

In the MS, zero pronouns are the most frequent type, and those of overt pronouns, descriptive NPs, and Full NPs are rare. In other words, the numbers of different kinds of Chinese anaphoric forms gradually decrease with the increasing of descriptive contents of anaphors in the MS, in that the degree of accessibility of the antecedent is relatively high in the MS.

The LS will lower the degree of accessibility of the antecedent to some degree. And hence the simplest Chinese anaphoric form, the zero pronoun, which is used to mark the highest accessibility of the antecedent, will thus be restricted in the LS. Moreover the anaphoric forms which are neither the simplest nor the most complicated—overt pronouns and descriptive NPs—are expected to occur most in the LS.

The GS can greatly lower the degree of accessibility of the antecedent, and therefore requires the anaphoric forms with many descriptive contents. Hence the numbers of different kinds of Chinese anaphoric forms should gradually increase with the descriptive contents of anaphoric forms increasing in the GS, which is accordant with the proportions of Chinese anaphoric forms in the corpus: the proportion of zero pronouns, overt pronouns, descriptive NPs, and Full NPs in the GS are 0%, 2.53%, 16.75%, and 63.14% respectively.

In general, the distributions of different kinds of Chinese anaphoric forms in distinct super-node structures strongly support the conceptual interpretations of

Chinese anaphoric forms in chapter 3. Moreover, the distributions can also provide an evidence for the impact of discourse structure on the uses of Chinese anaphoric forms.

### 4.3.2 Distributions of Anaphoric Forms Based on the Super-node Structures and the AN-pairs

This thesis has proposed that the super-node structures and the AN-pairs will interact on the accessibility of the antecedent and further determine the anaphoric form. So this section will compare all distributions of all kinds of Chinese anaphoric forms in the super-node structures and the AN-pairs, and further have an overall analysis on the corpus data and the conceptual interpretations of Chinese anaphoric forms. Below is the detailed distribution of Chinese anaphoric forms in the super-node structures and the AN-pairs.

**Table 4.13 The Distribution of Chinese anaphoric forms In the Super-node Structures and the Pairs of the Antecedent and the Anaphor**

| DS | The AN-pairs | ZPs | OPs | DesNPs | FNs |
|---|---|---|---|---|---|
| MS | Strong Continuation | 1965<br>97.18% | 7<br>1.04% | 0<br>0% | 0<br>0% |
| | Weak Continuation | 4<br>0.20% | 219<br>32.64% | 0<br>0% | 2<br>0.26% |
| | Smooth Shift | 32<br>1.58% | 72<br>10.73% | 11 5.42% | 0<br>0% |
| | Rough Shift | 0<br>0% | 18<br>2.68% | 2<br>0.98% | 0<br>0% |
| | Distant Link | 0<br>0% | 0<br>0% | 30 14.78% | 0<br>0% |
| LS | Strong Continuation | 21<br>1.04% | 280<br>41.73% | 13 6.40% | 25<br>3.19% |
| | Weak Continuation | 0<br>0% | 55<br>8.20% | 19 9.36% | 14<br>1.79% |
| | Short Link | 0<br>0% | 0<br>0% | 60 29.55% | 55<br>7.01% |
| | Distant Link | 0<br>0% | 3<br>0.45% | 34 16.75% | 193<br>24.62% |

| DS | The AN-pairs | ZPs | OPs | DesNPs | FNs |
|---|---|---|---|---|---|
| GS | Strong Continuation | 0<br>0% | 9<br>1.34% | 10 4.93% | 11<br>1.40% |
| | Weak Continuation | 0<br>0% | 8<br>1.19% | 7<br>3.45% | 76<br>9.69% |
| | Smooth Shift | 0<br>0% | 0<br>0% | 6<br>2.96% | 57<br>7.27% |
| | Rough Shift | 0<br>0% | 0<br>0% | 10 4.93% | 195<br>24.87% |
| | Short Link | 0<br>0% | 0<br>0% | 1<br>0.49% | 9<br>1.15% |
| | Distant Link | 0<br>0% | 0<br>0% | 0<br>0% | 147<br>18.75% |
| | | 2022<br>100% | 671<br>100% | 203 100% | 784<br>100% |

It seems that the distributions of Chinese anaphoric forms in Table 4.13 are disorganized in the corpus. If only viewed from the discourse structure, there is no restriction on the occurrence of various Chinese anaphoric forms. If only viewed from the pairs of the antecedent and the anaphor, there is no one-to-one relation between Chinese anaphoric forms and the AN-pairs.

But a strong tendency of different uses of Chinese anaphoric forms can be achieved based on the parallel comparisons from the horizontal as well as vertical perspectives based on the interaction between the super-node structures and the AN-pairs. Based on the horizontal comparison, the chief Chinese anaphoric forms to be used in a kind of the AN-pairs of a super-node structure can be obtained; and moreover the chief uses of a kind of Chinese anaphoric forms in different AN-pairs of different super-node structures can be obtained based on the vertical comparison. In Strong Continuation of the MS, for instance, the uses of zero pronouns occupy the dominant position either from the horizontal or the vertical perspective, and consequently zero pronouns should be typically used to encode the accessibility of the antecedent rendered by Strong Continuation of the MS. But it is different in Weak Continuation of the MS. In Weak Continuation of the MS the uses of overt pronouns take the dominant position from the horizontal perspective but just are a kind of common uses from the vertical perspective, hence overt pronouns should be mostly used to encode the accessibility of the antecedent rendered from Weak Continuation of the MS and some other AN-pairs.

It can be seen that the parallel comparison in Table 4.13 can clearly differentiate the different uses of various Chinese anaphoric forms. For example, both the zero pronouns and the overt pronouns can occur in Strong Continuation from the pairs of the antecedent and the anaphor, but their occurring super-node structures are distinct: the zero pronouns mostly occur in Strong Continuation of the MS, while the overt pronouns often occur in Strong Continuation of the LS.

Moreover, the above distributions of Chinese anaphoric forms in the corpus should be compared with the expected distributions in the conceptual interpretations of Chinese anaphoric forms, so that the validity of the conceptual interpretations of Chinese anaphoric forms in this thesis can be attested. The following is the detail comparison between them. Since there is the difference between the chief uses and peripheral uses of each kind of Chinese anaphoric uses, the AN-pairs marked with "*" is the chief.

**Table 4.14 The Comparison between the Corpus Distributions of Chinese anaphoric forms and Their Conceptual interpretations**

| Chinese | Expected Patterns | | Detail Distributions in the Corpus | | | |
|---|---|---|---|---|---|---|
| anaphoric forms | DS | AN-pairs | Numbers | % | Numbers | % |
| Zero Pronouns | MS | Strong Continuation* | 1965 | 97.18% | 1965 | 97.18% |
| Overt Pronouns | MS | Weak Continuation* | 219 | 32.64% | 626 | 93.3% |
| | | Smooth Shift | 72 | 10.73% | | |
| | LS | Strong Continuation* | 280 | 41.73% | | |
| | | Weak Continuation | 55 | 8.20% | | |
| Descriptive NPs | MS | Smooth Shift | 11 | 5.42% | 173 | 85.22% |
| | | Rough Shift* | 2 | 0.98% | | |
| | | Distant Link* | 30 | 14.78% | | |
| | LS | Weak Continuation | 19 | 9.36% | | |
| | | Short Link* | 60 | 29.55% | | |
| | | Distant Link | 34 | 16.75% | | |
| | GS | Strong Continuation* | 10 | 4.93% | | |
| | | Weak Continuation | 7 | 3.45% | | |

| Chinese anaphoric forms | Expected Patterns | | Detail Distributions in the Corpus | | | |
|---|---|---|---|---|---|---|
| | DS | AN-pairs | Numbers | % | Numbers | % |
| Full NPs | LS | Distant Link | 193 | 24.62% | 677 | 86.35% |
| | GS | Weak Continuation | 76 | 9.69% | | |
| | | Smooth Shift* | 57 | 7.27% | | |
| | | Rough Shift* | 195 | 24.87% | | |
| | | Short Link* | 9 | 1.15% | | |
| | | Distant Link* | 147 | 18.75% | | |

Viewed from the above table, it can be found that different Chinese anaphoric forms are distinct in the chief AN-pairs with the super-node structures, and moreover the uses of various Chinese anaphoric forms in the corpus all support the conceptual interpretations of Chinese anaphoric forms in chapter 3.

According to Table 4.14, 97.18% of zero pronouns in the corpus, 93.3% of overt pronouns, 85.22% of descriptive NPs, and 86.35% of Full NPs are consistent with the conceptual interpretations of Chinese anaphoric forms of this thesis respectively. In other words, most of zero pronouns and overt pronouns in the corpus can be rightly interpreted by the conceptual analysis of Chinese anaphoric forms in chapter 3. And a great number of descriptive NPs and Full NPs in the corpus can support the interpretations of Chinese anaphoric forms in chapter 3, though there is a small part of them which cannot be accounted for.

In general, the corpus data of Chinese anaphoric forms fully support the interpretations of Chinese anaphoric forms discussed in chapter 3. Hence, it can be concluded that different Chinese anaphoric forms are to mark distinguished domains of the accessibility continuum of the antecedent. Zero pronouns are to mark a special domain of the accessibility continuum of the antecedent, which only includes the highest degree of accessibility resulted from Strong Continuation of the MS and is the reference of all other Chinese anaphoric forms. Overt pronouns are to mark the domain which is lightly deviated from the highest accessibility and which includes a number of the degrees of accessibility mainly resulted from Weak Continuation of the MS and Strong Continuation of the LS. Descriptive NPs are to mark the domain which is heavily deviated from the highest accessibility and which includes the degrees of accessibility chiefly rendered by Rough Shift of the MS, Distant Link of the MS, Short Link of the LS, and Strong Continuation of the GS. And Full NPs are to mark the domain which is much heavily deviated from the highest accessibility and in which the accessibility is mainly rendered by the Shift and the Link AN-pairs of the GS.

## 4.4 Summary

In this chapter, I have undertaken a corpus-based study on uses of Chinese anaphoric forms and made a comparison between the corpus data and the interpretations of Chinese anaphoric forms.

This chapter has firstly investigated the distributions in the corpus of all Chinese anaphoric forms in super-node structures and the AN-pairs, and then compared all their distributions with the conceptual interpretations of Chinese anaphoric forms proposed in chapter 3. Based on the above corpus-based analysis, it is concluded that the corpus data of Chinese anaphoric forms strongly support the interpretations of Chinese anaphoric forms as outlined in chapter 3.

# Chapter 5 A Brief Comparison

This chapter will give some further discussion on the interpretations of Chinese anaphoric forms in this thesis, and further compare different approaches to anaphoric forms so that the explanatory power of the interpretations of Chinese anaphoric forms in this thesis can be more clearly revealed.

## 5.1 Advantages of the Interpretations of Chinese Anaphoric Forms in This Thesis

This thesis has interpreted Chinese anaphoric forms from the conceptual perspective as well as from the corpus perspective, and the corpus data of Chinese anaphoric forms well supports the conceptual interpretations. I think the distinctive uses of Chinese anaphoric forms can be well interpreted in this thesis due to these three aspects.

Firstly, this thesis has fully analyzed the factors which can impact the accessibility of the antecedent and further affect the uses of Chinese anaphoric forms.

Four main factors are posed in this thesis: discourse structure, the topicality, the saliency, and referential distance. Those four main factors have been mentioned in some previous research on Chinese anaphoric forms, but they have not all been taken into account in most of the previous research on Chinese anaphora. As a consequence, the distinctive uses of different Chinese anaphoric forms cannot be interpreted due to the partial perception on the main factors which can affect the accessibility of the antecedent.

Secondly, this thesis has clearly revealed how the main factors impact the accessibility of the antecedent and affect the uses of Chinese anaphoric forms.

The previous research on Chinese anaphoric forms has strived to find out how various factors affect the accessibility of the antecedent. But it is so regretful that the impacts of various factors on the accessibility of the antecedent have not been rightly or thoroughly revealed in the previous research, and consequently different uses of Chinese anaphoric forms cannot be rightly interpreted.

The most improved factor in this thesis is discourse structure. Discourse structure has been proposed that it can affect the uses of Chinese anaphoric forms in most of the previous research. But how the discourse structure affects the uses of Chinese anaphoric forms has not been clearly revealed in the previous research, in that the discourse structure is too complicated to be figured out.

This thesis has analyzed the discourse structure from a new way. This thesis firstly explores the structure of Chinese discourses in the generative framework and obtains a complete discourse structure. Based on the complete discourse structure, this thesis further distinguishes three kinds of super-node structures: the Minimal Structure, the Local Structure, and the Global Structure.

The distinction between those three kinds of super-node structures is very important for the interpretations of Chinese anaphoric forms, in that they can differently and greatly affect the accessibility of the antecedent. According to the analysis of this thesis, the impacts of other three factors except discourse structure—the topicality, the salience, and referential distance—are relatively easy to determine. But if the impact of discourse structure on the accessibility of the antecedent has not been rightly and clearly revealed, the impacts of the topicality, the salience, and referential distance on the accessibility of the antecedent will be easily confused. As proposed in this thesis, the impacts of the topicality, the salience, and referential distance are realized as the pairs of the antecedent and the anaphor, and moreover the accessibility of the antecedent is affected by the interactions between discourse structure and the pairs of the antecedent and the anaphor. A same kind of pairs of the antecedent and the anaphor can occur in different super-node structures. But since the super-node structures also can impact the accessibility of the antecedent, the same kind of the

AN-pairs in different super-node structures will result in different degrees of accessibility of the antecedent. Hence if there is no distinction between different super-node structures, the apparently same but actually different Chinese anaphora from the AN-pairs cannot be rightly differentiated, and the uses of different Chinese anaphoric forms consequently cannot be rightly interpreted. Some previous research even argues that there are some overlaps of the uses between different Chinese anaphoric forms, but they are actually different based on the analysis of this thesis.

Thus, the distinction between those three kinds of super-node structures is important for the interpretations of Chinese anaphoric forms. This thesis has clearly distinguished those three kinds of the super-node structures, and then provides a solid foundation for the interpretations of Chinese anaphoric forms.

Thirdly, this thesis has clearly revealed the correlation between the accessibility of the antecedent and Chinese anaphoric forms.

The correlation between the accessibility of the antecedent and Chinese anaphoric forms is crucial for the interpretations of Chinese anaphoric forms in the accessibility framework. The previous research all tries to find out the correlation between them. But the previous research has just suggested some general statements rather than the clear description on the correlation between the accessibility of the antecedent and Chinese anaphoric forms, in that the previous research has not provided a solution for the mismatch between the accessibility of the antecedent and Chinese anaphoric forms.

This thesis has solved the mismatch between the accessibility of the antecedent and the anaphor. This thesis proposes that all different degrees of accessibility of the antecedent can comprise an accessibility continuum and that Chinese anaphoric forms are to mark distinct domains of the continuum, in that not any different degrees of accessibility of the antecedent will result in the change of people's cognitive status which will require different Chinese anaphoric forms. Furthermore this thesis finds out the clear correlation between Chinese anaphoric forms and the distinct domains of the accessibility of the antecedent.

It can be indicated from the above discussions that this thesis has analyzed various Chinese anaphoric forms more fully and more thoroughly. And this thesis can thus achieve the more appropriate interpretations on the uses of Chinese anaphoric forms.

## 5.2 A Brief Comparison of Some Prominent Interpretations on Chinese Anaphoric Forms

This thesis has fully interpreted various Chinese anaphoric forms from the conception as well as the corpus perspective so far. In order to better understand the interpretations of Chinese anaphoric forms in this thesis, this section will compare the interpretations of Chinese anaphoric forms of this thesis with some prominent interpretations of the previous research from the theoretical perspective and from the instantiated perspective.

Since there are three representative theories on anaphoric forms: Centering Theory, Accessibility Theory, and Discourse Representation Theory, I will now chiefly compare the approach taken here with the interpretations of those other theories.

### 5.2.1 A Theoretical Comparison

This thesis has interpreted various Chinese anaphoric forms chiefly through the super-node structures on discourse structure and the pairs of the antecedent and the anaphor on topicality, salience, and referential distance. We can see that the interpretations of Chinese anaphoric forms in this thesis are different from the interpretations of the previous research. But there are some similarities.

Previous research in the accessibility framework mainly attempts to determine some rules and then to rank different discourse entities on the degree of accessibility, based on which different ranked entities are correlated with different anaphors. Concretely speaking, a number of discourse entities is regarded as the possible antecedents and then are then ranked according to some rules. And the ranked entities are correlated with some kind of anaphoric forms based on the mediation between them.

The interpretations of Chinese anaphoric forms of this thesis are actually the same as the interpretations of the previous research from the basic assumption. But this thesis succeeds in ranking many different discourse entities.

As is well known, there are many factors which can affect the accessibility of the antecedent. As accessibility is a matter of cognitive status, it is hard to determine the precise impact of different factors on the accessibility of the antecedent. Hence it is very difficult to give a precise ranking order for discourse entities on the strength of accessibility alone.

Rather than to precisely rank different discourse entities, this thesis aims to analyze the interaction between different factors on the accessibility of the antecedent. According to the interaction, this thesis also can obtain some hierarchies on the accessibility of the antecedent and moreover obtain the right correlation between the accessibility of the antecedent and Chinese anaphoric forms.

In short, the interpretations of Chinese anaphoric forms of this thesis and the interpretations of the previous research are similar in some ways, but the specific application and the proposals are different, and the interpretations are consequently different as well.

### 5.2.2 An Instantiated Comparison

This part will use some examples to show why the approach taken here is more plausible than the previous approaches. The representative interpretations of the previous research on anaphoric forms include the interpretations by CT, AT, and DRT. Meanwhile, two interpretations on anaphoric forms based on AT are taken into account: one is the interpretations based on Ariel (1990), and the other is the interpretations based on Y. Xu (2004). Here are the detail comparisons.

(5.1) $C_1$. Dajin$_i$ diaozhuan shenzi,

$C_2$. Ø$_i$ he Niang bing pai zhe gui zai yiqi,

$C_3$. yi gu suansuan de, nuannuan de ziwei yong man ta$_i$ de xiongwo.

'Dajin turned over his body, and kneeled with his mother together. A saline but warm feeling is full of his heart.'

There are two kinds of Chinese anaphoric forms in the example (5.1): the zero pronoun in (5.1$C_2$) and the overt pronoun *ta* in (5.1$C_3$). The interpretations of CT, Ariel (1990), Y. Xu (2004), DRT, and this thesis on the uses of Chinese anaphoric forms in (5.1) will be illustrated in sequence.

**Table 5.1 The Interpretations of CT on Chinese anaphoric forms in (5.1)**

| Text | Centers | Anaphors Interpretations of CT |
|---|---|---|
| $C_1$ | $C_f$: Dajin, shenzi<br>$C_p$: Dajin<br>$C_b$: undefined | / |
| $C_2$ | $C_f$: Ø (=Dajin), Niang<br>$C_p$: Ø (=Dajin)<br>$C_b$: Ø (=Dajin)<br>$C_t$: Continue | CT Prediction (Pronoun Rule): **Successful**<br>To reveal the anaphoric form: **Failed** |
| $C_3$ | $C_f$: ziwei, xiongwo, ta(=Dajin)<br>$C_p$: ziwei<br>$C_b$: ta(=Dajin)<br>$C_t$: Retain | CT Prediction (Pronoun Rule): **Successful**<br>To reveal the anaphoric form: **Failed** |

**Table 5.2 The Interpretations of Ariel (1990) on Chinese anaphoric forms in (5.1)**

| Text | AN Accessibility | Anaphors Interpretations of Ariel (1990) |
|---|---|---|
| $C_1$ | / | / |
| $C_2$ | $A_n$: Dajin($C_1$)<br>Highest Accessibility | Ariel's(1990) Prediction ( the Zero Pronoun): **Successful** |
| $C_3$ | $A_n$: Ø=(Dajin)($C_2$)<br>Highest Accessibility | Ariel's(1990) Prediction ( the Overt Pronoun): **Failed** |

**Table 5.3　The Interpretations of Y. Xu (2004) on Chinese anaphoric forms in (5.1)**

| Text | Antecedent Treatment | Anaphors Interpretations of Xu (2004) |
|---|---|---|
| $C_1$ | / | / |
| $C_2$ | $A_n$: Dajin($C_1$)<br>Highest Accessibility<br>The First Expected Topic | Y. Xu's(2004)　Prediction (the Zero Pronoun): **Successful** |
| $C_3$ | $A_n$: Ø=(Dajin)($C_2$)<br>Highest Accessibility<br>The First Expected Topic | Y. Xu's(2004)　Prediction (the Overt Pronoun): **Failed** |

**Table 5.4　The Interpretations of DRT on Chinese anaphoric forms in (5.1)**

| Text | DRT Proposals | Anaphors Interpretations of DRT |
|---|---|---|
| $C_1$ | x y z u v w j k | |
| $C_2$<br>$C_3$ | Dajin (x)<br>Shenzi(y)<br>Diaozhuan(x,y)<br>Ø(u)<br>Niang (v)<br>Gui(u, with v)<br>u=x<br>ziwei (w)<br>Ta(k)<br>Ta de Xiongwo(j)<br>k=u<br>Yongman(w,j) | √　The antecedents of the anaphors both are accessible for the anaphors.<br><br>×　DRT cannot tell the different uses between the zero pronoun in $C_2$ and the overt pronoun in $C_3$. |

**Table 5.5 The Interpretations of This Thesis on Chinese anaphoric forms in (5.1)**

| Text | AN-pairs | Anaphors Interpretations of This Thesis |
|---|---|---|
| $C_1$ | / | / |
| $C_2$ | $A_s$: MS<br>$A_n$: +T, +S, +C<br>$A_r$: +T, +S<br>$A_p$: Strong Continue | Anaphor Prediction (the Zero Pronoun): **Successful** |
| $C_3$ | $A_s$: MS<br>$A_n$: +T, +S, +C<br>$A_r$: +T, -S<br>$A_p$: Weak Continue | Anaphor Prediction (the Overt Pronoun): **Successful** |

**Table 5.6 The Comparison of Different Interpretations on Chinese anaphoric forms in (5.1)**

| Anaphors | CT | Ariel (1990) | Y. Xu (2004) | DRT | This Thesis |
|---|---|---|---|---|---|
| Ø($C_2$) | Partly Successful | Successful | Successful | Partly Successful | Successful |
| ta($C_3$) | Partly Successful | Failed | Failed | Partly Successful | Successful |

It can be viewed from Table 5.1-5.6 that Chinese anaphoric forms in (5.1) cannot all be rightly interpreted by the previous interpretations but can be interpreted by the interpretations of Chinese anaphoric forms in this thesis. The main reason is that the variations of the anaphor on the topicality and the salience have not been considered in the previous research. This thesis argues that the variations of the anaphor on the topicality and the salience also can affect the accessibility of the antecedent and further affect the uses of Chinese anaphoric forms, which makes the interpretations of Chinese anaphoric forms of this thesis can provide a correct interpretation of the uses of two Chinese anaphoric forms in (5.1).

(5.2) $C_1$.<u>Niang</u>$_i$ xing xiao，

$C_2$. <u>Ø</u>$_i$ meiyou ming。

$C_3$. Nanren jiao Xiangde,

$C_4$. renmen bian jiao <u>ta$_i$</u> Xiangde nvren, Xiangde laopo, Xiangde jiali de, Xiangde xifu.

"She has the surname Xiao, but hasn't the last name. Since the name of her husband is Xiangde, she is called Xiangde nv ren, Xiangde laopo, Xiangde jiali de, Xiangde xifu."

There are also two Chinese anaphoric forms in (5.2) which occur in (5.2 $C_2$) and (5.2 $C_4$) respectively. The anaphoric forms are also the zero pronoun and the overt pronoun *ta*. The detailed interpretations of various proposals on them are illustrated in below.

**Table 5.7 The Interpretations of CT on Chinese anaphoric forms in (5.2)**

| Text | Centers | Anaphors Interpretations of CT |
|---|---|---|
| $C_1$ | $C_f$ : Niang, xiao<br>$C_p$: Niang<br>$C_b$: undefined | / |
| $C_2$ | $C_f$: Ø(=Niang)<br>$C_p$: Ø(=Niang)<br>$C_b$: Ø(=Niang)<br>$C_t$: Continue | Pronoun Rule: **Successful**<br>To reveal the anaphoric form: **Failed** |
| $C_3$ | $C_f$ : nanren, Xiangde<br>$C_p$: nanren<br>$C_b$: undefined(a new segment) | / |
| $C_4$ | $C_f$ : renmen, ta, Xiangde nvren, Xiangde laopo, Xiangde jiali de, Xiangde xifu<br>$C_p$: renmen<br>$C_b$: undefined(a new segment) | Pronoun Rule: **Failed**<br>To reveal the anaphoric form: **Failed** |

**Table 5.8 The Interpretations of Ariel (1990) on Chinese anaphoric forms in (5.2)**

| Text | AN Accessibility | Anaphors Interpretations of Ariel (1990) |
|---|---|---|
| $C_1$ | / | / |
| $C_2$ | $A_n$: Niang($C_1$)<br>Highest Accessibility | Ariel's(1990) Prediction (the Zero Pronoun): **Successful** |
| $C_3$ | / | / |
| $C_4$ | $A_n$: Ø=(Niang)($C_2$)<br>Highest Accessibility | Ariel's(1990) Prediction (the Overt Pronoun): **Failed** |

**Table 5.9 The Interpretations of Y. Xu (2004) on Chinese anaphoric forms in (5.2)**

| Text | Antecedent Treatment | Anaphors Interpretations of Xu (2004) |
|---|---|---|
| $C_1$ | / | / |
| $C_2$ | $A_n$: Niang($C_1$)<br>Highest Accessibility<br>The First Expected Topic | Y. Xu's(2004) Prediction (the Zero Pronoun): **Successful** |
| $C_3$ | / | / |
| $C_4$ | $A_n$: Ø=(Niang)($C_2$)<br>Highest Accessibility<br>The Second Expected Topic | Y. Xu's(2004) Prediction (the Overt Pronoun): **Successful** |

**Table 5.10 The Interpretations of DRT on Chinese anaphoric forms in (5.2)**

| Text | DRT Proposals | Anaphors Interpretations of DRT |
|---|---|---|
| $C_1$ | x y z u v h i w j k | |
| $C_2$ | Niang (x) | √ The antecedents of the anaphors both are accessible for the anaphors. |
| $C_3$ | Xiao(y) | |
| $C_4$ | Xing(x,y) | |
| | Ø(u) | |
| | Ming (v) | × DRT cannot tell the different uses between the zero pronoun in $C_2$ and the overt pronoun in $C_4$. |
| | Mciyou(u, v) | |
| | u=x | |
| | Nanren(h) | |

| Text | DRT Proposals | Anaphors Interpretations of DRT |
|---|---|---|
| | Xiangde(i)<br>Jiao(h,i)<br>Renmen (w)<br>XiangDe Nvren, Xiangde laopo,<br>Xiangde jiali de, Xiangde xifu(j)<br>Ta(k)<br>k=u<br>Jiao(w,k,j) | |

**Table 5.11　The Interpretations of This Thesis on Chinese anaphoric forms in (5.2)**

| Text | AN-pairs | Anaphors Interpretations of This Thesis |
|---|---|---|
| $C_1$ | / | / |
| $C_2$ | $A_s$: MS<br>$A_n$: +T, +S, +C<br>$A_r$: +T, +S<br>$A_p$: Strong Continue | Anaphor Prediction (the Zero Pronoun):<br>**Successful** |
| $C_3$ | / | / |
| $C_4$ | $A_s$: LS<br>$A_n$: +T, +S, -C<br>$A_r$: +T, -S<br>$A_p$: Strong Continue | Anaphor Prediction (the Overt Pronoun):<br>**Successful** |

**Table 5.12　The Comparison of Different Interpretations on Chinese anaphoric forms in (5.2)**

| Anaphors | CT | Ariel (1990) | Y. Xu (2004) | DRT | This Thesis |
|---|---|---|---|---|---|
| Ø($C_2$) | Partly Successful | Successful | Successful | Partly Successful | Successful |
| Ta($C_4$) | Failed | Failed | Successful | Partly Successful | Successful |

It can be viewed from Table 5.7-5.12 that the zero pronoun and the overt pronoun *ta* in (5.2) also cannot be adequately interpreted by the CT, AT, and DRT.

The main reason is that different super-node structures have not been differentiated in the previous research. This thesis has distinguished three kinds of super-node structures—the MS, the LS, and the GS. And the same variations of Chinese anaphora on topicality, salience, and referential distance could be encoded by different kinds of Chinese anaphoric forms due to the occurrence in different kinds of super-node structures. The example (5.2) is such an illustration.

(5.3) $C_1$. Dajin$_i$ hen you chuxi.

$C_2$. Huifu gaokao na nian, ta$_i$ kao jin Beijing de na suo mingpai daxue,

$C_3$. quanxian ta$_i$ kao le di yi ming.

"Dajin was outstanding. He was admitted to the famous university in Beijing, and he ranked No. 1 in the whole county, while the university entrance examination was resumed."

There are still two Chinese anaphoric forms in (5.3) which both are the overt pronouns *ta*s in different clauses. The detailed interpretations on them are given below.

**Table 5.13 The Interpretations of CT on Chinese anaphoric forms in (5.3)**

| Text | Centers | Anaphors Interpretations of CT |
|---|---|---|
| $C_1$ | $C_f$: Dajin<br>$C_p$: Dajin<br>$C_b$: undefined | / |
| $C_2$ | $C_f$: ta (=Dajin)、daxue<br>$C_p$: ta (=Dajin)<br>$C_b$: ta (=Dajin)<br>$C_t$: Continue | CT Prediction (Pronoun Rule): **Successful**<br>To reveal the anaphoric form: **Failed** |
| $C_3$ | $C_f$: quanxian、ta、di yi ming<br>$C_p$: quanxian<br>$C_b$: ta (=Dajin)<br>$C_t$: Retain | CT Prediction (Pronoun Rule): **Successful**<br>To reveal the anaphoric form: **Failed** |

**Table 5.14 The Interpretations of Ariel (1990) on Chinese anaphoric forms in (5.3)**

| Text | AN Accessibility | Anaphors Interpretations of Ariel (1990) |
|---|---|---|
| $C_1$ | / | / |
| $C_2$ | $A_n$: Dajin($C_1$)<br>Highest Accessibility | Ariel's(1990) Prediction (the Overt Pronoun):<br>**Failed** |
| $C_3$ | $A_n$: ta=(Dajin)($C_2$)<br>Highest Accessibility | Ariel's(1990) Prediction (the Overt Pronoun):<br>**Failed** |

**Table 5.15 The Interpretations of Y. Xu (2004) on Chinese anaphoric forms in (5.3)**

| Text | Antecedent Treatment | Anaphors Interpretations of Xu (2004) |
|---|---|---|
| $C_1$ | / | / |
| $C_2$ | $A_n$: Dajin($C_1$)<br>Highest Accessibility<br>The First Expected Topic | Y. Xu's(2004) Prediction (the Overt Pronoun): **Failed** |
| $C_3$ | $A_n$: ta=(Dajin)($C_2$)<br>Highest Accessibility<br>The First Expected Topic | Y. Xu's(2004) Prediction (the Overt Pronoun): **Failed** |

**Table 5.16 The Interpretations of DRT on Chinese anaphoric forms in (5.3)**

| Text | DRT Proposals | Anaphors Interpretations of DRT |
|---|---|---|
| $C_1$ | x y u v w j k | |
| $C_2$<br>$C_3$ | Dajin (x)<br>Youchuxi(x)<br>Ta(y)<br>Nasuo Mingpai Daxue(u)<br>Nanian (v)<br>Kaojin(y, u at v)<br>y=x<br>Quanxian(w) | √ The antecedents of the anaphors both are accessible for the anaphors.<br>× DRT cannot tell the uses of the overt pronouns in $C_2$ and $C_3$. |

| Text | DRT Proposals | Anaphors Interpretations of DRT |
|---|---|---|
| | Ta(j)<br>Diyiming(k)<br>Kao(j,i at w)<br>j=y | |

**Table 5.17 The Interpretations of This Thesis on Chinese anaphoric forms in (5.3)**

| Text | AN-pairs | Anaphors Interpretations of This Thesis |
|---|---|---|
| $C_1$ | / | / |
| $C_2$ | $A_s$: LS<br>$A_n$: +T, +S, +C<br>$A_r$: +T, +S<br>$A_p$: Strong Continue | Anaphor Prediction (the Overt Pronoun):<br>**Successful** |
| $C_3$ | $A_s$: MS<br>$A_n$: +T, +S, +C<br>$A_r$: +T, -S<br>$A_p$: Weak Continue | Anaphor Prediction (the Overt Pronoun):<br>**Successful** |

**Table 5.18 The Comparison of Different Interpretations on Chinese anaphoric forms in (5.3)**

| Anaphors | CT | Ariel (1990) | Y. Xu (2004) | DRT | This Thesis |
|---|---|---|---|---|---|
| ta($C_2$) | Partly Successful | Failed | Failed | Partly Successful | Successful |
| ta($C_3$) | Partly Successful | Failed | Failed | Partly Successful | Successful |

Viewed from Table 5.13-5.18, it is seen that neither of the two Chinese anaphoric forms in (5.3) can be interpreted by the previous research, while they can be predicted by the proposals of this thesis. The main reasons that the previous research cannot rightly interprct those two Chinese anaphoric forms are that the impacts of the super-node structures and the variations of the anaphor on the topicality and the salience have not been recognized. This thesis has clearly revealed the effect of the super-node structures and has moreover taken the variations of the anaphor on topicality and saliency into account in analyzing different uses of Chinese anaphoric forms. As a result, this thesis can rightly interpret all kinds of Chinese anaphoric forms.

In general, the above three examples all indicate that the interpretations of Chinese anaphoric forms of this thesis can overcome some limitations of the previous interpretations on anaphoric forms and further well interpret distinctive uses of various Chinese anaphoric forms.

## 5.3 Summary

This chapter gives a brief comparison, with examples, between the approaches taken in this thesis and those prominent approaches of the previous research. Our approach is shown to be more powerful than those of the previous research.

# Chapter 6 Conclusions

## 6.1 Summary

Through the study presented in the previous chapters, this thesis has well explained the behaviors of various Chinese anaphoric forms from the point of view of information accessibility. The basic claim is that although all discourse entities could serve as an antecedent, different types of antecedents vary in the degree of accessibility and consequently can have different types of impact on uses of Chinese anaphoric forms.

There are two main aspects in this thesis: a) what factors can affect the accessibility of the antecedent in Chinese discourses; and b) how the factors affect the accessibility of the antecedent in Chinese discourses.

Four main factors are proposed to affect the accessibility of the antecedent: types of discourse structure, status of the topicality, the salience in cognition, and referential distance. Their domain of effects varies.

The factor with the most impact is discourse structure. This thesis analyzes discourse structure in a generative framework. It is assumed that the basic unit of discourse is the clause, and there are different hierarchies among clauses. Different clause hierarchies constitute what I call discourse structures. The most basic clausal relationships can be defined in terms of three types of information relations what I call higher structures: Coordination, Subordination, and Binary. Coordination refers to two or more discourse units where the information conveyed is continuous and additive. Subordination refers to two or more discourse units where information from subsequent units adds any new information to that of the initial unit. Finally, Binary relation refers to two discourse units where different information is connected with an explicit or implicit relation. Higher structures can be applied recursively to combine various discourse units, no matter whether discourse units are the basic units or not, until a whole discourse is generated. And thus, the whole structure of a discourse is established, which is realized as DISCOURSE PARSE TREE (DPT).

Based on the DPT, there are three kinds of super-node structures which affect the accessibility of the antecedent: the Minimal Structure (MS), the Local Structure (LS), and the Global Structure (GS). A Minimal Structure contains one and only one kind of higher structures outlined above which links all different clauses included by it, and hence the antecedent is highly accessible for an anaphor given the anaphora occurs in a MS. A Local Structure is a combination of two or more kinds of higher structures in which all clauses included by it share one discourse segment topic, and therefore the antecedent will not be accessible so highly than that in the MS due to a longer hierarchical distance and a looser information correlation. A Global Structure is defined as a set of higher structures without a shared topic, and hence the antecedent is naturally lowly accessible for the anaphor due to no structural as well as information relation between two clauses in a GS.

Whether or not an antecedent or an anaphor is topical in discourse can affect the accessibility of the antecedent and the anaphoric forms in subsequent clauses. A topical referent can be either clause-based or segment-based, depending on the scope of the structure. A discourse segment topic is a shared referent among multiple clauses in a local structure, while a clause-level topic is either the subject of the current clause or a related referent shared by the current clause and the preceding clause.

Whether or not the antecedent or the anaphor is most salient in a clause can affect the accessibility of the antecedent. Cognitive saliency is a relative concept, which operates mainly in the Local and Minimal Structures. It refers to the status of a referent among a group of referents of a clause. The most salient referent is typically found in the subject position of a clause.

Referential distance between the antecedent and the anaphor also can affect the accessibility of the antecedent. Whether the antecedent and the anaphor occur in two connective clauses is the main factor: in general the more intervening clauses between the antecedent and the anaphor, the less accessible the antecedent is and the less likely they co-refer.

Among those four main factors, discourse structures such as the super-node structures can greatly affect the accessibility of the antecedent. The other three factors, topicality, saliency, and referential distance, are regarded as properties related to the pairs of the antecedent and the anaphor (AN-pairs) which can reveal the inference load of discourse anaphora and discourse coherence.

Concretely speaking, discourse structure affects the accessibility of the antecedent through three kinds of super-node structures: the MS, the LS, and the GS. Those three kinds of super-node structures categorize all kinds of antecedents into three sets which are distinguished in the accessibility. The accessibility hierarchy of those three sets of antecedents is as follows: the Antecedents in the MS > the Antecedents in the LS > the Antecedents in the GS. What is on the left is the super-node structure in the hierarchy, which is more accessible to the antecedent for the anaphor.

Topicality, saliency, and referential distance affect the accessibility of the antecedent through the pairs of the antecedent and the anaphor. Six kinds of AN-pairs are proposed in this thesis: Strong Continuation, Weak Continuation, Smooth Shift, Rough Shift, Short Link, and Distant Link, which has implication for the use of Chinese anaphoric forms. Strong Continuation refers to the AN-pairs in which both the antecedent and the anaphor are the topics and most salient, and the antecedent is recent for the anaphor. Weak Continuation refers to the AN-pairs in which both the antecedent and the anaphor are the topics, but not both of them are most salient or the antecedent is not recent for the anaphor. Smooth Shift refers to the AN-pairs in which one of the antecedent and the anaphor is the topic, but both of them are most salient or the antecedent is recent for the anaphor. Rough shift refers to the AN-pairs in which one of the antecedent and the anaphor is the topic, but not both of them are most salient or the antecedent is not recent for the anaphor. Short Link refers to the AN-pairs in which neither the antecedent nor the anaphor is the topic but the antecedent is recent for the anaphor. And Distant Link refers to the AN-pairs in which neither the antecedent nor the anaphor is the topic, moreover the antecedent is not recent for the anaphor. The antecedents in those AN-pairs can be ranked on the accessibility: the Antecedents in Strong Continuation > the Antecedents in Weak Continuation > the Antecedents in Smooth Shift > the Antecedents in Rough Shift > the Antecedents in Short Link > the Antecedents in Distant Link.

With regard to the overall relationship between super-node structures and the AN-pair types, we can say that they interact with each other and together impact the accessibility of the antecedent. For any given type of super-node structure, the accessibility of the antecedent will decrease gradually from Strong Continuation, Weak Continuation, Smooth Shift, Rough Shift, Short Link, to Distant Link. And for any given type of AN-pair from the antecedent to the anaphor, the degree of accessibility of the antecedent will decrease gradually from Minimal Structure, Local Structure, to Global Structure. However, it is found that discourse (super-node) structure plays a major role in the use of Chinese anaphoric forms, and AN-pair types may manifest in different types of accessibility in the antecedent due to the impact of the discourse structure. Thus, the same kind of AN-pair may manifest in different degrees of accessibility in the antecedent and different kinds of AN-pairs may share a similar degree of accessibility in the antecedent, due to the discourse structures in which they appear.

With the three types of super-node structures and six types of AN-pair, there are a total of 18 possible combinations. This thesis analyzes the impacts of all eighteen possibilities involving the interaction between the super-node structure and the AN-pairs on the accessibility of the antecedent, and proposes the accessibility domain to solve the mismatch between the degrees of accessibility of the antecedent and the types of Chinese anaphoric forms.

Thus, four distinctive patterns about all 18 combinations are established to interpret Chinese anaphoric forms: 1) Strong Continuation in Minimal Structure typically result in the use of a zero pronoun; 2) Weak Continuation in a Minimal Structure and Strong Continuation in a Local Structure typically result in the use of an overt pronoun; 3) Rough Shift and the Link in a Minimal Structure, Short Link in a Local Structure, and Strong Continuation in a Global Structure often result in the use of a descriptive NP; and finally, 4) Other than the Continuation, all other AN-pairs in a Global Structure can result in the use of a full NP. And other combinations not mentioned above have untypical uses on Chinese anaphoric forms due to the fuzzy property of the accessibility continuum of the antecedent.

Based on the above discussion, an Accessibility Marking Hierarchy in Chinese anaphors is established, as schematized below: zero pronouns > overt pronouns (the third-person pronoun / the definite pronouns) > descriptive NPs > full NPs. In this scheme, zero pronouns mark the highest degrees of accessibility of the antecedent, and overt pronouns mark the higher degrees, and descriptive NPs mark the intermediate degrees, and full NPs mark the lower even the lowest degrees.

Our conceptual analysis of Chinese anaphoric forms is backed up by results from a corpus-based study. Using a collection of modern written Chinese texts of over two hundred thousand words, this study found that the use of Chinese anaphoric forms in the eighteen combinations involving super-node structures and the AN-pairs matches the four distinct patterns outlined above.

In summary, this thesis provides a comprehensive account of the use of Chinese anaphoric forms from the point of view of information accessibility.

## 6.2 Contributions

The major contribution of this thesis is that for the first time we have identified a set of super-node structures based on discourse structure and AN-pair types and their interaction. Moreover, we illustrate how this interaction impacts the use of the four major types of Chinese anaphoric forms.

Discourse structure is an important factor which can impact the accessibility of the antecedent and affect the uses of Chinese anaphoric forms. But the impact of discourse structure on the accessibility of the antecedent has not been clearly and rightly revealed before. This thesis for the first time analyzes discourse structure of Chinese in a generative framework, and for the first time again, proposes three kinds of super-node structures which can clearly present the impact of discourse structure on the accessibility of the antecedent.

The pairs of the antecedent and the anaphor of this thesis are also the first time to be proposed in all research on Chinese anaphoric forms. The pairs of the antecedent and the anaphor are mainly concerned with the behaviors of the antecedent and the anaphor on the topicality, the salience, and referential distance. The topicality, the salience, and referential distance all are commonly considered to affect the uses of Chinese anaphoric forms in the previous research on Chinese anaphoric forms. The main difference between this thesis and the previous research on those three factors is that this thesis takes into account the behaviors of the anaphor on them. By combining the behaviors of the antecedent with those of the anaphor on the topicality, the salience, and referential distance, the pairs of the antecedent and the anaphor are accordingly achieved. It can be indicated that the pairs of the antecedent and the anaphor can reveal the impact of the topicality, the salience, and referential distance on the accessibility of the antecedent more fully, in that they can reveal the inference load from the anaphor to the antecedent.

Naturally how discourse structure and the pairs of the antecedent and the anaphor interact on the accessibility of the antecedent and Chinese anaphoric forms should be further explored in this thesis. After the detail conceptual analysis, this thesis poses a solution to solve the mismatch between the degrees of accessibility of the antecedent and Chinese anaphoric forms and gives an explicit correlation between Chinese anaphoric forms and the patterns of Chinese anaphora involving the interaction between discourse structure and the pairs of the antecedent and the anaphor, which also contribute to the better interpretations of Chinese anaphoric forms in this thesis.

# References

[1] Aissen J. (1999). Markedness and subject choice in optimality theory. Natural Language and Linguistic Theory 17: 673-711.

[2] Almor A. and Veena A. N. (2007). The form of referential expressions in discourse. Language and Linguistics Compass 1/1-2: 84-99.

[3] Aoun J. (1985). A grammar of anaphora. Cambridge: The MIT Press.

[4] Ariel M. (1990). Accessing noun-phrase antecedents. London: Routledge.

[5] Ariel M. (2001). Accessibility theory: an overview. In Ted Sanders, Joost Schilperoord and Wilbert Spooren (eds.): Text representation: Linguistic and psycholinguistic aspects. Amsterdam: John Benjamins.

[6] Arnold J. (1998). Reference form and discourse patterns. Ph. D. thesis, Stanford University.

[7] Asher N. (1993). Reference to abstract objects in discourse. Dordrecht: Kluwer.

[8] Asher N. and Lascarides A. (1994). Intentions and information in discourse. In Pustejovsky J. (ed.): Proceedings of the thirty-second meeting of the association for computational linguistics. San Francisco: Morgan Kaufmann: 35-41.

[9] Asher N. and Lascarides A. (1998). The semantics and pragmatics of presupposition. Journal of Semantics, 15: 239-299.

[10] Asher N. and Lascarides A. (2003). Logics of conversation. New York: Cambridge University Press.

[11] Beaver D. (1999). The logic of anaphora resolution. In Dekker P. (ed.): Proceedings of the 12th Amsterdam Colloquium, University of Amsterdam.

[12] Beaver D. (2004). The optimization of discourse anaphora. Linguistics and

Philosophy 27: 3-56.

[13] Brennan S., Friedman M. and Pollard C. (1987). A centering approach to pronouns. Proceedings of the 25th annual meeting of the association for computational linguistics. Cambridge, Mass., Association for Computational Linguistics.

[14] Blutner R. (2000). Some aspects of optimality in natural language interpretation. Journal of Semantics 17(3): 189-216.

[15] Brown G. and Yule G. (1983). Discourse analysis. Cambridge: Cambridge University Press.

[16] Byron D. and Stent A. (1998). A preliminary model of centering in dialog, URCS Technical Report #687, August.

[17] Chen P. (2004). Identifiability and definiteness in Chinese. Linguistics: 42(6): 1129-1184.

[18] Chen P. (2009). Aspects of referentiality. Journal of Pragmatics: 41: 1657-1674.

[19] Chierchia G. (1992). Anaphora and dynamic binding. Linguistics and Philosophy, 15: 111-183.

[20] Chierchia G. (1995). Dynamics of meaning: anaphora, presupposition, and the theory of grammar. Chicago: The University of Chicago Press.

[21] Chu C. C. (1998). A discourse grammar of Mandarin Chinese. New York : P. Lang.

[22] Cui Y., Hu Q., Pan H. and Hu J. (2006). Zero anaphora resolution in Chinese discourse. In Gelbukh A. (ed.): CICLing 2006, Lecture notes in computer science 3878: 245-248. Berlin Heidelberg: Springer-Verlag.

[23] Davidson D. (1967). The logical form of action sentences. In Pescher N. (ed.): The logical form of action sentences. Pittsburgh: University of Pittsburgh Press: 81-95.

[24] Dowty D. and Jacobson P. (1989). Agreement as a semantic phenomenon. Proceeding of the Eastern States Conference on Linguistics (ESCOL '88). Columbus: The Ohio State University, Department of Linguistics: 95-108.

[25] Forbes K. and Miltsakasi E. (2002). Empirical studies of centering shifts and cue phrases as embedded segment boundary markers. In Kaiser E. (ed.):

Penn Working Papers in Linguistics 7(2): Current work in linguistics: 39-57.

[26] Givon T. (1976). Topic, pronoun and grammatical agreement. In Li C. N. (ed.): Subject and Topic. New York: Academic Press.

[27] Givon T. (1979). Syntax and Semantics. Vol. 12: Discourse and Syntax. New York: Academic Press.

[28] Givon T. (1983). Topic continuity in discourse analysis: a quantitative cross-linguistic study. Amsterdam: John Benjamins Publishing Company.

[29] Gordon P. C. (1999). Naming versus referring in the selection of words. Behavioral and Brain Sciences, 22: 44.

[30] Gordon P. C. and Hendrick R. (1998). The representation and processing of coreference in discourse. Cognitive Science, 22: 389-424.

[31] Gordon P. C. and Hendrick R. (1998). Dimensions of grammatical coreference. Proceedings of the Twentieth Annual Conference of the Cognitive Science Society: 424-429. Hillsdale, NJ: Lawrence Erlbaum Associates.

[32] Gordon P. C. and Hendrick R. (1998). Implicit causality, negation, and models of discourse. Proceedings of the Twentieth Annual Conference of the Cognitive Science Society: 430-435. Hillsdale, NJ: Lawrence Erlbaum Associates.

[33] Gordon P. C. and Hendrick R. (1999). Comprehension of coreferential expressions. Meeting of the Association for Computational Linguistics: Proceedings of the Workshop on the Relation of Discourse/Dialogue Structure and Reference: 82-89, New Brunswick, NJ: Association for Computational Linguistics.

[34] Gordon P. C. and Hendrick R. (1999). Non-definite NP anaphora: A reappraisal. In Gruber M. C., Higgins D., Olson K. S. and Wysocki T. (eds.): CLS34: The main session: 95-210. Chicago: Chicago Linguistics Society.

[35] Gordon P. C., Grosz B. J. and Gilliom L. A. (1993). Pronouns, names and the centering of attention in discourse. Cognitive Science, 17: 311-348.

[36] Grimshaw J. (1997). Projection, heads and optimality. Linguistic Inquiry 28

(3): 373-422.

[37] Grosz B. J., Aravind Joshi K. and Weinstein S. (1995). Centering: a framework for modelling the local coherence of discourse. In Computational Linguistics, 21/2: 203-225.

[38] Grosz B. J. and Sidner C. L. (1986). Attentions, intentions and the structure of discourse. Computational Linguistics, 12: 175-204.

[39] Gundel J. K., Hedberg N. and Zacharski R. (1993). Cognitive status and the form of referring expressions in discourse. Language 69:274-307.

[40] Gundel J. K., Hedberg N. and Zacharski R. (1997). Topic-comment structure, syntactic structure and prosodic tune. Helsinki: Workshop on Prosody and Grammar in Interaction: 13-15.

[41] Gundel J. K. (1991) Topic, Focus, and the Grammar-Pragmatics Interface.

[42] Heim I. (1982). The semantics of definite and indefinite noun phrases. Ph.D. thesis, MIT.

[43] Hitzeman J. and Poesio M. (1998). Long-distance pronominalisation and global focus. Proc. ACL-98, Montreal, August.

[44] Hu J. and Pan H. (2000). Deriving the subject-object asymmetry in topicalization. Preceeding of the International Symposium on Topic and Focus 2000.

[45] Hu J. and Pan H. (2001). Processing local coherence of discourse in Centering Theory. Proceedings of the 15th Pacific Asia Conference on Language, Information and Computation. Hong Kong: City University of Hong Kong.

[46] Hu J. and Pan H. (2002). Focus tracking in English and Chinese discourse. Proceedings of National Conference on Modern Linguistics, Beijing, China.

[47] Hu Q. (2007). A corpus-based study on zero anaphora resolution in Chinese discourse. Ph. D. thesis, City University of Hong Kong.

[48] Huang Y. (1994). The syntax and pragmatics of anaphora: a study with special reference to Chinese. Cambridge: Cambridge University Press.

[49] Huang Y. (2000). Anaphora: A cross-linguistic study. Oxford and New York: Oxford University Press.

[50] Jackendoff R. S. (1990). Semantic structures. Cambridge, Mass.: MIT Press.

[51] Jackendoff R. Johnson, Laird, P. N. (1983). Mental models. Cambridge, Mass.: Harvard University Press.

[52] Jiang P. (2004). Syntactic and discourse features of zero anaphora-with specific reference to its resolution in Chinese. Ph. D. thesis, Shanghai International Studies University.

[53] Jiang Y. (2000). Hanyu tiaojian ju de weishi jieshi (On counterfactual interpretation of Chinese conditionals). In Mei Fang, Bojiang Zhang and Guangan Shi (eds.): Yufa Yanjiu he Tansuo, 10). (Analyses and Explorations in [Chinese] Grammar), Vol. 10, Beijing: Commercial Press: 257-279.

[54] Jiang Y., Pan H. and Zou C. (1997). On the semantic content of noun phrases. In Xu, L. J. (ed.): The Referential Properties of Chinese Noun Phrases. Paris: Ecole des Hautes Estudes en Sciences Sociales: 3-24.

[55] Kamp H. (1981). A theory of truth and discourse representation. In J. Groenendijk, T. Janssen, and M. Stokhof (eds.): Formal Methods in the Study of Language. Amsterdam: Mathematical Centre: 277-322.

[56] Kamp H. and Reyle U. (1993). From discourse to logic: introduction to model-theoretic semantics of natural language, formal logic and discourse representation theory. Kluwer Academic.

[57] Keenan E. L. and Comrie B. (1977). Noun phrase accessibility and universal grammar. Linguistic Inquiry 8(1): 63-99.

[58] Keenan E. L. and Hawkins S. (1987). The psychological validity of the accessibility hierarchy. In Keenean E. (ed.): Universal Grammar: 15 essays (60-85). Routledge, London.

[59] Kibble R. (1999). $C_b$ or not $C_b$? Centering theory applied to NLG. Proceedings of ACL'99 Workshop on Discourse and Reference Structure, University of Maryland.

[60] Kratzer, A. (1995). Stage-level and individual-level predicates. In Carlson G. and Pelletier J. (eds.): The Generic Book: 125-175. The University of Chicago Press, Chicago, IL.

[61] Krifka Manfred, Pelletier Francis Jeffry, Carlson Gregory N., Meulen Alice ter, Link Godehard, and Chierchia Gennaro (1995). Genericity: an introduction. In Gregory N. Carlson and Francis Jeffry Pelletier (eds.): The Generic Book: 1-124. Chicago and London: University of Chicago Press.

[62] Langacker R. W. (1988). A usage-based model. In Rudzka-Ostyn Brygida (ed.): Topics in Cognitive Linguistics. Amsterdam/Philadelphia: John Benjamins: 127-161.

[63] Langacker R. W. (1987). Foundations of Cognitive Grammar, Vol. 1. Stanford: Stanford University Press.

[64] Langacker R. W. (1991). Foundations of Cognitive Grammar, Vol. 2. Stanford: Stanford University Press.

[65] Langacker R. W. (1993). Reference-point constructions. Cognitive Linguistics 4: 1-38.

[66] Langacker R. W. (1996). Conceptual grouping and pronominal anaphora. In Fox B. (ed.): Studies in Anaphora. Amsterdam/ Philadelphia: John Benjamins Publishing Company: 333-378.

[67] Langacker R. W. (2000). A dynamic usage-based model. In Barlow M. and Kemmer S. (eds.): Usage-based Models of Language. Stanford, Calif.: CSLI Publications: 1-63.

[68] Langacker R. W. (2008). Cognitive grammar: a basic introduction. New York: Oxford University Press.

[69] Li C. N. and Thompson S. A. (1991). Mandarin Chinese: a functional reference grammar. Berkeley: University of California Press.

[70] Li S., Li W. and Zhou C. L. (2005). Research on Chinese ellipsis recovering based on discourse representation theory. Proceeding of 17th IEEE International Conference on Tools with Artificial Intelligence.

[71] Liu F. H. (1997). Scope and specificity. Amsterdam/Philadelphia: John Benjamins.

[72] Lyons J. (1995). Linguistics semantics: an introduction. Cambridge: Cambridge University Press.

[73] Paul W. (2002). Sentence-internal topics in Mandarin Chinese: the case of object preposing. Language and Linguistics 3(4): 695-714.

[74] Pearson J., Stevenson R. and Poesio M. (2001). The effects of animacy, thematic role, and surface position on the focusing of entities in discourse. Proc. of the 1st Workshop on Cognitively Plausible Models of Semantic Processing, Edinburgh, July.

[75] Poesio M. (2004). An empirical investigation of definiteness. In Kepser S. (ed.): Proc. of the International Conference on Linguistic Evidence, Tübingen, January. University of Tübingen, SFB: 441.

[76] Poesio M., Cheng H., Henschel R., Hitzeman J., Kibble R. and Stevenson R. (2000). A corpus-based investigation of centering theory. Proc. of the ACL, Hong Kong, October.

[77] Poesio M., Stevenson R. and J. Hitzeman. (1997). Global focus and pronominalization. In Jurafsky D. and Regier T. (eds.): First Conference on Computational Psycholinguistics, Berkeley.

[78] Poesio M., Stevenson R., Eugenio B. and Hitzeman J. M. (2004). Centering: a parametric theory and its instantiations. Computational Linguistics. Vol. 30, No. 3: 309-369.

[79] Polanyi L. (2003). The linguistic structure of discourse. In Eborah Schiffrin, Deborah Tannen, Heidi Ehernberger Hamilto (eds.): The Handbook of Discourse Analysis. Oxford: Blackwell Publishing: 265-281.

[80] Prince E. F. (1981). Toward a taxonomy of given-new information. In Cole P. (ed.): Radical Pragmatics. New York: Academic Press.

[81] Prince E. F. (1992). The ZPG letter: subjects, definiteness, and information-status. In Thompson S. and Mann W. (eds.): Discourse description: diverse analyses of a fund raising text: 295-325. Philadelphia/ Amsterdam: John Benjamins B.V.

[82] Pu M. M. (1995). Anaphoric patterning in English and Mandarin narrative production. Discourse Processes (19): 279-300.

[83] Pu M. M. (1998). Zero anaphora and grammatical relations in Chinese. In Givon T. (ed.): Grammatical relations: A Functionalist Perspective, Amsterdam/Philadelphia: John Benjamin's Publishing Company: 281-321.

[84] Reboul A. (1997). What (if anything) is accessibility? A relevance-oriented criticism of Ariel's accessibility theory of referring expressions. In

Connolly J. H. et al. (eds.): Discourse and Pragmatics in Functional Grammar: 91-108, Berlin/NY, de Gruyter.

[85] Roberts C. (1986). Modal subordination, anaphora, and distributivity. Ph. D. thesis, University of Massachusetts at Amherst.

[86] Roberts C. (1989). Modal subordination and pronominal anaphora in discourse. Linguistics and Philosophy 12(6): 683-721. In Reprinted in Javier Gutierrez-Rexach (ed.): Semantics: Critical concepts in linguistics, Routledge, (2003).

[87] Roberts C. (1996). Anaphora in intensional contexts. In Lappin S. (ed.): The Handbook of Contemporary Semantic Theory, Basil: Blackwell: 215-246.

[88] Roberts C. (1998a). Focus, the flow of information, and universal Grammar. In Culicover P. and McNally L. (eds.): The Limits of Syntax, Academic Press.

[89] Roberts C. (1998b). Information structure: towards an integrated formal theory of pragmatics. In Jae H. Y. and Kathol A. (eds.): OSUWPL Volume 49: Papers in Semantics, (1996). The Ohio State University Department of Linguistics.

[90] Roberts C. (2002). Demonstratives as definites. In Van Deemter K. and Kibble R. (eds.): Information Sharing: Reference and Presupposition in Language Generation and Interpretation. CSLI Press, Stanford: 89-136.

[91] Roberts C. (2003). Uniqueness in definite noun phrases. Linguistics and Philosophy 26: 287-350.

[92] Roberts C. (2005). Pronouns as definites. In M. Reimer and Bezuidenhout A. (eds.): Descriptions and Beyond. Oxford University Press.

[93] Roberts L. (1993). How Reference Works: Explanatory Models for Indexicals, Descriptions, and Opacity. SUNY Press.

[94] Shen Y. (2002). The semantics and pragmatics of bare noun phrases in Chinese. Ph. D. thesis, City University of Hong Kong.

[95] Shi D. (2000). Topic and topic-comment in Mandarin Chinese. Language 69: 274-307.

[96] Smith C. S. (2003). Modes of Discourse: The Local Structure of Texts.

New York: Cambridge University Press.

[97] Tao H. (1996). Units in Mandarin conversation: prosody, discourse, and grammar. Amsterdam/ Philadelphia: John Benjamins Publishing Company.

[98] Tetreault J. R. (2001). A corpus-based evaluation of centering and pronoun resolution. Computational Linguistics Vol. 27 No. 4: 507-520.

[99] Tsao F. (1990). Sentence and clause structure in Chinese: a functional perspective. Taipei: Student Book, Co.

[100] Van Hoek K. (1995). Conceptual reference points: A cognitive grammar account of pronominal anaphora constraints. Language 71/2: 310-340.

[101] Walker M. A. (1989). Evaluating discourse processing algorithms. Proceedings of the 27th ACL: 251-261.

[102] Walker M. A. (1996). Limited attention and discourse structure. Computational Linguistics, 22(2): 255-264.

[103] Walker M. A. (2000). Toward a model of the interaction of centering with global discourse structure, verbum.

[104] Walker M. A., Joshi A. K. and Prince E. F. (eds.) (1998). Centering theory in discourse. Oxford: Oxford University Press.

[105] Wang D. (2006). Anaphora resolution in Chinese from the centering perspective. Ph. D. thesis, Beijing Normal University.

[106] Webber B. L. (1978). A formal approach to discourse anaphora. Doctoral dissertation, Harvard University, Cambridge, MA. Garland Press.

[107] Weng Y. (2006). Zero anaphora in Chinese narratives from a cognitive perspective. Ph. D. thesis, Fudan University, China.

[108] Xu J. (2002). Noun-anaphora in Chinese texts. Ph. D. thesis, City University of Hong Kong.

[109] Xu J. (2005). Associative anaphora in Chinese discourse. Chinese Language Vol. 3: 195-204.

[110] Yeh C. L., Chen Y. C. (2000). Zero anaphora resolution in Chinese with shallow parsing. Journal of Chinese Language and Computing Vol. 17: 41-56.

[111] 陈平．话语分析说略[J]．语言教学与研究，1987（3）：4～18.

[112] 陈平．现代语言学研究：理论、方法与事实[M]．重庆：重庆出版社，

1991.
[113] 崔玉珍. 篇章语义信息框架与汉语篇章连贯性[D]. 北京：北京大学，2004.
[114] 丁国旺. 汉语语篇中人称代词、光杆名词和零代词回指加工的可及性研究[D]. 上海：华东师范大学，2005.
[115] 丁启阵. 现代汉语"这"、"那"的语法分布[J]. 世界汉语教学，2003（2）：27～38.
[116] 方经民. 现代汉语第三人称代词指称及其语境制约[J]. 当代语言学，2004（3）：236～247.
[117] 高卫东. 语篇回指的功能意义解析[M]. 上海：上海交通大学出版社，2008.
[118] 胡壮麟. 语篇的衔接与连贯[M]. 上海：上海外语教育出版社，1994.
[119] 姜望琪. 主题、主位与篇章——评《篇章回指的功能语用探索》[J]. 外语教学与研究，2005，37（5）：387～392.
[120] 蒋严，潘海华. 形式语义学引论[M]. 北京：中国社会科学出版社，1998.
[121] 李瑟. 基于语篇表述理论的汉语第三人称代词预指功能与回指确认研究[D]. 北京：北京交通大学，2005.
[122] 梁鲁晋. 语篇中回指的功能[M]. 厦门：厦门大学出版社，2008.
[123] 廖秋忠. 现代汉语中动词的支配成分的省略[J]. 中国语文，1984（4）：241～247.
[124] 廖秋忠. 廖秋忠文集[M]. 北京：北京语言学院出版社，1992.
[125] 刘丹青. 汉语类指成分的语义属性和句法属性[J]. 中国语文，2002（5）：411～422.
[126] 吕叔湘，朱德熙. 语法修辞讲话[M]. 北京：北京开明书店，1951.
[127] 马文. 会话中的回指修正研究——基于汉语戏剧会话的语料分析[M]. 济南：山东大学出版社，2007.
[128] 苗兴伟. 语篇向心理论述评[J]. 当代语言学，2003（2）：149～157.
[129] 潘海华. 篇章表述理论概说[J]. 国外语言学，1996（3）：17～26.
[130] 秦洪武. 第三人称代词在深层回指中的应用分析[J]. 当代语言学，2001（1）：55～64.
[131] 沈园. 汉语光杆名词词组语义及语用特点研究[M]. 上海：复旦大学出版社，2005.

[132] 王晓斌，周昌乐. 基于语篇表述理论的汉语人称代词的消解研究[J]. 厦门大学学报（自然科学版），2004（1）：203～225.
[133] 王秀卿，王广成. 汉语光杆名词短语的语义解释[J]. 现代外语，2008（2）：131～140.
[134] 王寅. 认知语言学与语篇分析[J]. 外语教学与研究，2003（2）：83～88.
[135] 徐赳赳. 叙述文中“他”的话语分析[J]. 中国语文，1990（5）：325～337.
[136] 徐赳赳. 话语分析二十年[J]. 外语教学与研究，1995（1）：14～18.
[137] 徐赳赳. 篇章中的段落分析[J]. 中国语文，1996（2）：81～91.
[138] 徐赳赳. 小句的概念和小句的划分. 转引自：钱军（ed.）：语言学：中国与世界同步：231～247，北京：外语教学与研究出版社，2003.
[139] 徐烈炯. 共性与个性[M]. 北京：北京语言文化大学出版社，1999.
[140] 徐烈炯，刘丹青. 话题与焦点新论[M]. 上海：上海教育出版社，2003.
[141] 徐烈炯，刘丹青. 话题的结构与功能[M]. 上海：上海教育出版社，2007.
[142] 许余龙. 汉英篇章中句子主题的识别[J]. 外国语，1996（6）：3～9.
[143] 许余龙. 英汉指称词语表达的可及性[J]. 外语教学与研究，32（5）：321～328.
[144] 许余龙. 语篇回指的认知语言学探索[J]. 外国语，2002（1）：28～37.
[145] 许余龙. 汉语主从间的回指问题[J]. 当代语言学，2005（2）：97～107.
[146] 许余龙. 篇章回指的功能语用探索——一项基于汉语民间故事和报刊语料的研究[M]. 上海：上海外语教育出版社，2004.
[147] 许余龙. 语篇回指实证研究中的数据库建设[J]. 外国语，2005（2）：23～29.
[148] 许余龙. 从回指确认的角度看汉语叙述体篇章中的主题标示[J]. 当代语言学，2005（2）：122～131.
[149] 许余龙. 向心理论的参数化研究[J]. 当代语言学，2008（3）：225～236.
[150] 许余龙，段嫚娟，付相君.“语句”与“代词”的设定对指代消解的影响——一项向心理论参数化实证研究[J]. 现代外语，2008（2）：111～120.
[151] 袁毓林. 话题化及相关的语法过程[J]. 中国语文，1996（4）：241～254.
[152] 张举栋. 不同文体中英汉指称词语可及性的对比研究[D]. 上海：上海海事大学，2005.

[153] 郑贵友. 汉语篇章语言学[M]. 北京：外文出版社，2002.
[154] 中国社会科学院语言研究所词典编辑室. 现代汉语词典[M]. 第 4 版. 北京：商务印书馆，2002.
[155] 周平. 可及性理论与前指现象[J]. 外语教学，2001，22（4）：3～8.
[156] 朱永生，严世清. 系统功能语言学多维思考[M]. 上海：上海外语教育出版社，2001.
[157] 邹崇理. 话语表现理论述评[J]. 当代语言学，1998（4）：20～31.